ECONOMIC IMPACT ANALYSIS

STUDIES IN APPLIED
REGIONAL SCIENCE 19

Editor-in-Chief
P. Nijkamp
Free University, Amsterdam

Editorial Board
Å. E. Andersson
University of Gothenburg, Gothenburg
W. Isard
Regional Science Institute, Philadelphia
L. H. Klaassen
Netherlands Economic Institute, Rotterdam
I. Masser
State University, Utrecht
N. Sakashita
Osaka University, Osaka

ECONOMIC IMPACT ANALYSIS: METHODOLOGY AND APPLICATIONS

Saul Pleeter, Editor

Martinus Nijhoff Publishing
Boston/The Hague/London

Distributors for North America:
Martinus Nijhoff Publishing
Kluwer Boston Inc.
160 Old Derby Street
Hingham, Massachusetts 02043

Distributors outside North America:
Kluwer Academic Publishers Group
Distribution Centre
P. O. Box 322
3300AH Dordrecht, The Netherlands

Library of Congress Cataloging in Publication Data

Main entry under title:

Economic impact analysis.

  (Studies in applied regional science; 19)
  Papers presented at a workshop held in Oxford, Ohio,
Apri. 13–15, 1977.
  Bibliography: p.
  Includes index.
  1. Regional economics—Mathematical models.
2. Interindustry economics—Mathematical models.
3. Regional planning—Evaluation. I. Pleeter,
Saul, 1944–   II. Series.
HT391.E32   330.9   79-25297

ISBN 0-89838-040-5

To Elizabeth—My wife, advisor, friend

CONTENTS

PREFACE

As a result of a contract awarded by the Construction Engineering Research Laboratory, U.S. Army Corps of Engineers, and the Environmental Protection Agency, a workshop on the methodology of economic impact analysis was held at Hueston Woods State Park Lodge in Oxford, Ohio, April 13-15, 1977. Leading researchers in regional modeling were gathered to take stock of current developments in the field and to put forth new ideas and directions for research. Also attending the workshops were individuals from various governmental agencies that use regional models and economic impact statements. Preliminary versions of the papers appearing in this volume served as focal points for discussions that have hopefully continued, stimulating further thinking of the problems addressed.

The objectives of the conference were not only to explore recent developments in methodology but also to expose users of economic impact analyses to a wide variety of models and applications and to acquaint academicians with the needs of users. The papers appearing in this volume represent only a portion of the output of this workshop.

A workshop such as the one at Hueston Woods can almost never be the product of one individual's efforts. Ravi Jain, Peter Cook, and Dwight Webster from the sponsoring agencies supported the concept of a workshop and provided encouragement and assistance in working through all of the myriad arrangements that are prerequisites for a successful meeting. Bob Miki and Ray Grimes helped formulate the program, the format of the sessions, and the selection of participants. Without the cooperation of these individuals there would not have been a workshop.

This volume, much like the workshop, is the joint product of many individual efforts. Especially deserving of note is Dennis Hanseman who was of invaluable assistance in the preparation of this manuscript.

INTRODUCTION

Frequently, policymakers are not aware of the relative advantages and limitations of alternative models for regional economic impact analysis. If there is a lack of familiarity with the richness of the various regional models, and if questions that need to be posed are not explicitly stated, inappropriate choices may be made. One remedial policy would be to expose the "users" of economic impact statements to a variety of regional models and their applications. The papers appearing in this volume are the result of a workshop that had this as one of its objectives.

This volume is divided into two parts: methodology and applications. This dichotomy is somewhat artificial, for each of the "applications" papers are based upon a specific methodology while many of the "methodology" papers have been or could be applied to particular problems. The location of each paper in the volume reflects the primary focus of the paper.

The first chapter presents an overview of the basic regional models. Conceptual and technical problems accompanying the implementation of these models provide a basis for evaluating many of the methodological issues presented in subsequent chapters.

The next two chapters deal with the methodology of the economic base model. Andrew Isserman's paper analyzes four alternative techniques for apportioning total employment into its basic and nonbasic components. Theoretical deficiencies in the techniques are presented and modifications suggested to improve their forecasting ability. Extensive empirical comparisons of the four techniques based upon previous studies and his own research highlight the deficiencies presented earlier and suggest avenues for further research.

Richard Pfister in chapter 3 presents an argument for the use of the minimum requirements technique for estimating exports originating in the tourist services industry. At present, the typical approach for estimating exports via an indirect method is to apply a single procedure, like location quotients, across every industrial category. Despite the many criticisms of minimum requirements, Pfister feels its use is appropriate in the case of tourist-serving industries where the idea of a minimum required production to serve the local population has some meaning. The balance of the paper is devoted to an empirical analysis of this proposition.

In chapter 4, Benjamin Stevens and Glynnis Trainer present some interesting work that has significant implications for the construction of nonsurvey and small-sample input-output models. The authors' evaluation of nonsurvey and small-survey techniques is based on a series of simulation experiments where a hypothetical matrix of technical coefficients is subjected to random errors of various orders of magnitude. After row and column constraints have been satisfied, total direct, indirect, and induced sectoral outputs together with overall output and wage multipliers are computed. Using Theil's U-statistic as the principal tool of comparison, the authors find that errors introduced in the interindustry matrix coefficients are considerably less important than errors in the regional purchase coefficients. Their analysis suggests that a reorientation of efforts in constructing these models should have considerable payoff.

Chapter 5 also concerns input-output methodology. Denise DiPasquale and Karen Polenske describe a multiregional input-output model and the calculation of output, employment, and income multipliers. They also contrast these multipliers with single region input-output and the aggregate Keynesian multipliers. The multiregional input-output model emphasizes the interrelatedness of a regional economy with other regional economies. Unlike other regional models which treat other regions as a homogeneous entity, this multiregion model explicitly considers trade flows among the regions. One advantage of this framework is that the multipliers derived are more comprehensive. They allow for feedback effects that have been ignored in single region models.

The title of chapter 6 gives a clear indication of the orientation of the author, Donald Ratajczak. Deficiencies in specifications of regional econometric models are a characteristic of previous efforts. These deficiencies, only partly excused by the paucity of regional data, are the result of the theoretical framework chosen by the model builder and of an inefficient use of data bases that are available at the regional level.

A region is, to a certain extent, a microcosm of the national economy, but there are important differences. First of all, a regional economy is a labor market — and labor market processes should be given increased importance in regional modeling especially since many historical series are available. Next, the economic problem of space is stressed in theoretical models of regional and urban economics and notably ignored in modeling these processes. Although many aspects of spatial behavior require a great deal of information that is not available, the implications of differential transportation costs and market areas can be provided for and thus used as adjustments to the more standard equations. Finally, one of the more interesting problems that current models have not been able to address is the differential cyclical responses of regional economics. Ratajczak argues that this essentially stems from adopting the usual neoclassical assumptions in constructing regional models. If one were to incorporate disequilibrium in some of the commodity and/or factor markets (nonprice responses to decreased demand, rigid money wages, inventory adjustments), the model can produce differential regional growth rates as well as cyclical variations. This paper is illustrative of some modifications to existing specifications and suggests further avenues for continued research.

The second half of the book, chapters 7–9, is devoted to applications of regional models. Norman Glickman's paper presents examples of the use of econometric models for economic impact analysis. Through the use of such models, analysts are able to capture both aggregate and disaggregate direct and indirect effects of exogenous shocks in a flexible and cost-effective way. Four case studies are discussed, based upon the Philadelphia Region Econometric Model, to illustrate the flexibility of these techniques. Glickman uses as examples the oil shortage, revenue sharing, local tax policies, and a reduction in defense spending.

In chapter 8, William Schaffer discusses the application of regional input-output models to economic impact analysis. His presentation distinguishes between two types of changes: structural change and change in final demand.

Structural change, not often considered, can occur in the model through new investment, changed marketing structure, public investment in social overhead capital, or the introduction of a new plant into the region. Schaffer demonstrates how these two categories of change can be incorporated in an input-output model using examples from the Georgia table and a simulation of the economic impact of baseball in Montreal.

The paper by Curtis Harris, chapter 9, briefly describes the methodology and some of the many uses of the Multiregional, Multi-Industry Forecasting Model. The model is both highly disaggregative and comprehensive. Disaggregation is along both geographic and industrial lines, with each of the 3,000 countries in the United States being observation units and industry detail provided for one hundred industries. This model differs from other econometric models in that it provides considerably more detail as well as having dynamic properties. It is designed to be used with Clopper Almon's U.S. input-output model which provides forecasts of industry output for the nation. Harris' model then allocates this total to each of the counties.

There have been numerous applications of this model to economic impact analysis. The areas in which major applications have been undertaken are transportation, communications, offshore oil and gas development, coal mining, public employment programs, natural gas cutbacks, and so on. Harris's paper describes the development of these impact analyses as well as detailing many of the problems involved.

I METHODOLOGY

1 METHODOLOGIES OF ECONOMIC IMPACT ANALYSIS: AN OVERVIEW

Saul Pleeter*

1.1 INTRODUCTION

There are two basic ingredients to an economic impact analysis: an estimate of the exogenous or differential stimulus that serves as the direct impact, and a model of the regional economy that will produce estimates of the indirect effects.[1] Perhaps due to increased demand for economic impact statements by various levels of government there has been a fairly dramatic increase in modeling efforts in recent years. Methodological innovations resulting from these research efforts have produced an almost infinite variety of models that resist categorization. Economic base multipliers are estimated with econometric techniques,[2] input-output models are treated as econometric models,[3] and hybrid models are constructed that may combine elements of economic base, econometric, and input-output models. [4] There are aggregate and disaggregate models of all types so that even the level of aggregation cannot serve as an alternative classifying variable.[5]

Recognizing these difficulties, and at the risk of being overly pragmatic, this overview presents three basic categories of models to represent the

*Associate Professor of Economics, University of Cincinnati.

essential features of numerous modeling efforts. These categories are economic base, econometric, and input-output models.

These models, typically used for economic impact analysis, vary considerably in terms of the detail presented and the data and effort required, as well as in their view of the causes of regional growth. While each of the models has desirable features, they also have significant drawbacks so that the choice of a model will depend upon the nature of the problem to be analyzed as well as the resources available. In order to understand the relationship between the problem to be investigated and the characteristics of these regional models, it is necessary to analyze the major conceptual and technical problems inherent in each model as well as data requirements and method(s) of implementation.

1.2 ECONOMIC BASE MODELS

1.2.1 Description

Economic base models dichotomize economic activity in a region into export and local service industries.[6] Economic base models view the local economy much like a household with a single wage earner. Household income and standard-of-living can only increase with increases in wages earned by the head. The counterpart to the single wage earner in economic base models is the export industry. Industries and establishments within the local economy that cause funds to flow in are considered to be export industries. These are the firms that sell their products to businesses and households outside the boundaries of the local economy. We also consider tourism facilities and federal and state government to be part of the export industry since they are responsible for money inflows. Local service industries, by contrast, sell their outputs only within the local economy.

Without "new" injections of funds to the local economy, the economy will be stagnant, since local service industries can only respond to changes in local economic conditions. External changes that result in an increase in export activity cause increases in payroll and employment in the export industries which are then transmitted to the local service sector. Further, the inflow of money causes activity in local services to change by a multiple of the original stimulus as the new influx of funds is spent and respent in the local economy. Recirculation continues until the leakages to the system, like imports, savings, and taxes, exhaust the amount of the initial influx. Similar, though opposite, effects occur in the case of a decrease in export activity.

Mathematically, we can express this model by

$$Y_L = C + I + X - M \qquad (1.1)$$

Income (Y_L) for the local economy is equal to the sum of consumption (C), investment (I), and government spending (G), plus exports (X) minus imports (M). The behavioral relationships governing the magnitudes of these variables can be given as

$$C = a_o + b\,Y_d \qquad (1.2)$$
$$Y_d = (1 - t)Y_L$$
$$I = I_o$$
$$G = G_o$$
$$X = X_o$$
$$M = mY_d$$

where b is the marginal propensity to consume, t is the marginal tax rate, Y_d is disposable income, and m is the marginal propensity to import. While imports and a portion of consumption expenditures are hypothesized to vary with changes in local disposable income, we assume, at least initially, that investment, government spending, exports, and a portion of consumption are unresponsive to any change in local economic conditions. That is,

$$a_o + I_o + G_o + Y_o = \bar{K} \qquad (1.3)$$

where $\bar{K}$ is some constant.

Substituting equations (1.2) and (1.3) into equation (1.1) and combining terms yields

$$Y_L[1 - (b - m)(1 - t)] = \bar{K} \qquad (1.4)$$

so that

$$Y_L = \frac{1}{1 - (b - m)(1 - t)} \cdot \bar{K} \qquad (1.4a)$$

Local income is determined by exogenous expenditures $\bar{K}$ and the marginal propensity to spend locally out of disposable income, $1 - (b - m)(1 - t)$. If any of the exogenous components in $\bar{K}$ were to change, local income would change according to

$$\frac{dY}{d\bar{K}} = k_o = \frac{1}{1 - (b - m)(1 - t)} \qquad (1.5)$$

This expression is termed the *economic base multiplier*.

If we were to allow for additional sources of growth, such as an induced change in investment, our model would become a bit more complex. For example, let

$$I = c + iY \qquad (1.6)$$

where i is the marginal propensity to invest. The multiplier could then be derived as

$$\frac{dY_L}{dK} = k_1 = \frac{1}{1 - (b - m)(1 - t) - i} \qquad (1.7)$$

Still other modifications would separate the various components of consumption, investment, and government, and include separate relationships describing the determinants of each source of demand. These modifications generally serve to increase k by lowering the leakages from the system. We will call multipliers derived from a model that allows for sources of regional growth in addition to changes in the exogenous components of demand, *first-order multipliers*.[7] This description of the economic base model is almost identical in structure to the Keynesian model of the determination of aggregate income and employment and to the international trade models.

1.2.2 Conceptual Problems

The economic base model can be characterized as a highly simplified general equilibrium model of a local economy. It assumes that the economy is initially in equilibrium and describes a new equilibrium position after the exogenous change has been transmitted through the system. Prices, wages, and technology are assumed constant, supply is perfectly elastic, and no changes in the distribution of income or resources are allowed for.

As a theory of regional growth, economic base models emphasize the "openness" of regional economies; that is, regional trade is considered to be the primary impetus for growth. The high degree of interrelatedness between the local economy and "the rest of the world" is based solely on a demand orientation. Exogenous changes in the demand for exports determine regional income and employment changes. In reality, export sales are not the only activity that responds to exogenous forces, even in the short run. Omission of these other exogenous influences from the model suggests that economic base studies are appropriate primarily for smaller regional economies where exports represent a larger proportion of total regional activity.

Clearly there are other "internal" causes of growth that would warrant inclusion in a more fully specified growth model. Investment expenditures or local government expenditures, for example, could cause income changes in the local economy. These additional sources of income change can be handled in an economic base model and have been illustrated in our description of first-order multipliers. Other internal changes in productivity, technology, population, urbanization, and agglomeration economies could also result in local income changes but are generally not incorporated in base models. In fact, implicit in this export-orientation is the notion that export sales are generated because of the region's comparative advantage. Consequently, any change in local economic structure, to the extent that it changes the economy's comparative advantage, can cause local income changes. These latter effects are longrun consequences and appropriately should not be considered in a model that has a shortrun orientation. In the shortrun, the assumption that internal adjustments will be made in a specific manner to export changes does not seem to be grossly unrealistic.

Another factor that argues for application of this methodology to smaller regions is the omission of "feedback" effects in the analysis. If exports increase, this leads to an increase in local income and imports. Imports are, however, another region's exports, and this increase in extra regional income could cause further changes in the demand for exports in the first region.

The economic base model ignores the supply side of the local economy, implicitly assuming that supply is perfectly elastic. This neglect of supply does not appear to be a serious defect if the exogenous stimulus is small relative to the size of the economy, or if the region itself is small. Given the degree of openness of a local economy and the migrational propensity of labor, an elastic supply would not be an unrealistic assumption. Capacity constraints will present problems to the degree that the local infrastructure is not capable of supporting the expansion. If energy, water, transportation facilities, and land for expansion are at full capacity prior to an increase in demand for exports, then we would expect price increases rather than an expansion in quantity.

Another criticism of the economic base model is its assumption of a relatively stable relationship between local consumption and income. Import substitution can distort this relationship since, with regional growth, goods and services that were previously imported tend to be provided locally. To the extent that this occurs, the local consumption-income relationship will be unstable over time. The omission of other factors such as wealth, permanent income, population, and the distribution of income may also result in an unstable consumption-income relationship.

While data on local wealth is unavailable, the influence of permanent income, the distribution of income, and population changes could be incorporated in the model. This would require the use of historical data, and there is some question as to whether the additional detail will yield nonmarginal changes given the likelihood that significant changes in these variables will not occur in a short time span. Significant changes in these factors, as well as structural change in the local economy, will cause changes in the magnitude of the economic base multiplier. Although initial formulations of this model assumed the multiplier to be stable and constant over time, Hildebrand and Mace (1950) and others have shown this assumption to be invalid.

An evaluation of the conceptual problems inherent in the economic base model would have to conclude that it is not an appropriate model for explaining longrun regional growth. However, the difficulties inherent in the model do not appear to be serious if the economic base model is considered to be a theory of income determination in the shortrun. Many of the problems can be reduced or eliminated by a more detailed analysis. Of the problems that remain, it is reasonable to assume that only insignificant bias will be introduced provided that the economic base model is appropriately applied. To lend further support for the use of the economic base model in shortrun applications, at least two studies have estimated that approximately 90 percent of the forecasted change occurs within a year.[8] If the impacts are realized within a short time horizon, the economic base model would be an appropriate methodology.

1.2.3 Technical Problems

1.2.3.1 Units of measurement. The economic base model, as presented, requires detailed information on the parameters of equation (1.1) in order to be operational. Our multiplier was given as:

$$k_o = \frac{1}{1 - (b - m)(1 - t)} \tag{1.8}$$

where $(b - m)$ is the marginal propensity to consume locally, b is the marginal propensity to consume, m is the marginal propensity to import, and t is the tax rate. Since detailed information on the above parameters is not generally available (or available only by survey), some transformations will have to be made in order to be useful to the researcher. If we assume that the marginal propensity to consume locally is equal to the average propen-

sity to consume and that consumption is proportional to income, we can re-
write the multiplier as:

$$k_o = \frac{1}{1 - (b-m)(1-t)} = \frac{1}{1 - \dfrac{\text{local consumption}}{\text{total consumption}}} =$$

$$= \frac{1}{1 - \dfrac{\text{local income}}{\text{total income}}} . \qquad (1.9)$$

Rearranging the terms in the denominator yields

$$k_o = \frac{\text{total income}}{\text{basic income}}. \qquad (1.9a)$$

Although income is used as a proxy for the variables of the model, other
variables such as employment, sales, and value-added could have been applied to the above equation.

Employment is the most frequently used unit of measurement for the
economic base model. In fact, the original work on the economic base
model formulated the multiplier as the ratio of basic (export) employment
to local service sector employment. The mathematical relationships previously described were introduced after the economic base model had become popular in the literature. Using employment as the unit of measurement is advantageous because the data is available and on a disaggregated
basis (four-digit SIC) for the larger local economies. In addition, employment forecasts or impacts are often requested by those parties commission-
ing the study. But the use of employment does have its drawbacks.

In particular the ratio of employment to income is neither constant nor
stable over time. Total jobs conveys no information about the relative distribution of skills and thus may mask underlying changes in wage levels. For
example, an employer may be able to substitute one $20,000 foreman for
two $10,000 operatives, with unchanged output. Although local income is
approximately the same, employment will show a net decrease. Increases in
labor productivity, on the other hand, will generate additional local income
at the same level of employment, thus distorting the relationship between
the two. In addition, the response of an employer to cyclical fluctuations
will vary by occupation and industry, with some employees (those with high
skills and specific human capital) being retained on the payroll even though
they contribute little to total production. This last effect suggests that marginal responses to external stimuli might differ from average responses so

that the use of more than one observation might be called for in calculating multipliers.

Income originating by sector (or value-added) has recently become available on a county basis from the Bureau of Economic Analysis, U.S. Department of Commerce, and could be applied to equation (1.1). However, these income values are quite aggregated and may introduce other problems (detailed next) in the analysis.

1.2.3.2 Identifying basic income or employment. In order to operationalize the model, it is necessary to determine how much of the region's total employment or income is devoted to basic activities. A problem exists in that most goods produced in the local economy are typically sold in both local and nonlocal markets. Of course, one could use a marketing survey to discover the allocation of sales by industry, but these surveys tend to be costly. As an alternative to a survey, a number of indirect methods have been proposed to approximate this allocation. These indirect methods include location quotients, minimum requirements, and the assumption approach.

Using employment as an example, location quotients compare the concentration of industry employment in a particular region with that of the nation. Since exports are assumed to be negligible for the nation, a region that has a greater percentage of its employment concentrated in an industry than does the nation must be producing for export since it has more than the average employment required to satisfy its domestic needs. Mathematically, the location quotient is derived according to:

$$\mathrm{LQ}_i = \frac{e_i}{e} \div \frac{E_i}{E} \quad (i = 1, 2, \ldots, s) \tag{1.10}$$

where lower case letters refer to employment in the region, and capital letters refer to national employment. The subscript i denotes the industry while letters without subscripts represent total employment.

If the location quotient is greater than unity, the region is an exporter for that commodity, while location quotients less than one indicate that the region is not satisfying its domestic requirements and must import the good. A location quotient equal to one states that the region is neither an importer nor an exporter. The proportion of employment that is devoted to the production of exports (assuming LQ_i is greater than 1) is given by:

$$\mathrm{ex}_i = e_i \left(\frac{\mathrm{LQ}_i - 1}{\mathrm{LQ}_i} \right) \tag{1.11}$$

with ex_i representing export employment for industry i. Location quotients compare the given region to an "average" region of the country and assume:

1. Consumer tastes and incomes are the same throughout the nation.
2. Production functions for each industry are identical in every region (equivalent to assuming that productivity and returns to scale are the same for each region).
3. Local demand is satisfied by local production.
4. The nation neither imports nor exports commodities.

While these assumptions may appear to be stringent, more recent research has attempted to make adjustments to the location quotient procedure. Isserman (1977a) has suggested modifications that incorporate national exports into a calculation of the employment-output base. Productivity and income differences are related to one another, and Mayer and Pleeter (1975) have recommended a procedure for adjusting location quotients to account for these differences. While little information is available on consumer tastes, a number of researchers have recommended more disaggregated comparisons, such as with other "similar" regions, as the basis for calculating location quotients.

The accuracy of location quotients has been questioned for still other reasons. Since location quotients identify net rather than gross exports, they tend to overestimate economic base multipliers. If imports were exogenous to the model (unrelated to local income), the use of net exports would be appropriate. However, in the model presented, and in most applications, imports are considered to be endogenous and therefore exports are underestimated. Isserman (1977b) has developed a bracketing procedure using location quotients and an approach developed by Mathur and Rosen (1974) in which multipliers derived by location quotients serve as an upper bound to the "true" multiplier.

Aggregated data also tend to mask the degree of exportation. For example, using location quotients for two-digit SIC code industries, where some of the four-digit industries are net exporters and some are net importers, could produce an estimate of zero net exports for the two-digit industry. Clearly the solution here is to use disaggregated data.

Sales data have also been used in economic base studies but since they typically involve double-counting, they distort the multiplier analysis.[9] Payroll data have also been recommended but since they do not include other factor payments, such as interest, profits, or rent, multipliers derived from this data base will tend to be larger.

What seems to be an appropriate solution to this problem is to adjust disaggregated employment values by the more aggregated income-originating variable. This would especially be desirable when multiperiod observations are used to derive multipliers.

Minimum requirements compare the given region to the "minimum" region of the country for each industry in order to calculate exports. Following a procedure developed by Ullman and Dacey (1960), a group of similar regions are used to calculate the percentage of total employment in each industry.[10] The minimum percentage across regions of employment for each industry is then considered to be the minimum required to satisfy domestic needs. Employment in excess of this minimum is export employment.

The assumptions behind the minimum requirements approach are:

1. Consumer tastes and incomes are the same throughout the nation.
2. Production functions for each industry are identical in every region.
3. Local demand is satisfied by local production.
4. Every city completely satisfies its own domestic needs.

While the first three assumptions for the minimum requirements approach are identical to those stated for location quotients, the fourth assumption is different. Since the minimum requirements city completely satisfies its own demand, every other city must be an exporter and, consequently, no city imports any goods. Ullman and Dacey postulated this approach as a replacement for location quotients. However, it appears that the minimum requirements approach has severe limitations and is subject to more severe criticisms than the approach it was to replace.

The assumption approach is rather simple to describe. Researchers allocate employment into basic and nonbasic by judgments concerning the market orientation of the products. Sometimes this procedure is accomplished on an "ad hoc" basis; at other times industry experts are consulted or sample surveys undertaken to produce this division. While the use of this approach has the virtue of being quick and inexpensive, it is usually inaccurate. One of the primary difficulties is that indirect exports are not considered. As an example of indirect exports, consider a major exporter like Procter and Gamble in Cincinnati. This firm manufactures and exports soaps, detergents, and toothpaste. Other firms in the area supply Procter and Gamble with packaging material for their products. Both survey and industry experts would reveal that the packaging firms have local markets and therefore should not be counted as export firms. However, since packaging firms supply important inputs to a product that is exported, they should appropriately be included in the export category. It should be noted that both location quotients and minimum requirements would count indirect exports in their analysis.

Another problem concerns enterprises that sell in both local and nonlocal markets. The assumption approach would generally categorize their employment into either one or the other category, but not both. While it is possible that errors made under this approach would be offsetting, in all probability a bias would be introduced into the analysis.

1.2.4 Implementation

If the questions being raised in an economic impact analysis concern highly aggregative variables such as total employment, income, and/or taxes, the forecast period is one to four years, answers are to be provided in six months or less, and the research budget is quite limited, then there is no question that an economic base model should be used. The virtue of an economic base model is its ease of implementation at moderate cost. While there is considerable variation in the complexity of previous studies, the variation does not reflect ambiguity as to the core of the methodology. Basic equations for the multiplier, location quotients (used to dichotomize employment), and the calculation of export employment are available in any number of textbooks. Data necessary for implementation of the model is modest and is available in published sources. An economic base model can be constructed by an individual with limited exposure to regional analysis and can be completed within six months at modest cost. In this basic model, industry detail cannot be provided. The same estimated total change is produced no matter which industry transmits the initial change.

Within the basic framework of the economic base model, modifications to existing procedures can be undertaken to address some of the conceptual problems outlined above. Location quotients based on disaggregated employment data and adjusted to account for national exports, regional productivity, and income differences would be an improvement. Disaggregation of employment data alleviates a significant problem inherent in more aggregative studies, namely the industry mix problem. (Although the industry mix problem would still exist, it would be less severe.) Another criticism of the model relates to the use of data for a single time period in calculating the multiplier. An appropriate method for handling this problem is to use more than one observation in calculating the multiplier. Applying regression analysis to multiperiod observations would capture trends inherent in the data and reduce the influence of extreme observations. The drawbacks to this suggestion are that it increases both the money and time costs of undertaking the study; and since exports are assumed to be measured with error, the estimated multiplier will be biased.[11]

1.3 ECONOMETRIC MODELS

1.3.1 Description

Econometric models are multiple-equation systems that attempt to describe the structure of a local economy and forecast aggregate variables such as income, employment, and output. There is no single theory of regional growth that is implicit in the development of these models. Rather, model builders generally take an eclectic approach and incorporate specifications that are specific to the region being analyzed. The Keynesian Open System is most often the theoretical framework for the development of an econometric model. The crucial distinction between the economic base and econometric models relates to the implementation and measurement of the structural relationships rather than their theories of regional growth. Econometric models employ time series data (rather than the typical single period reference of economic base models) to construct the model and estimate the hypothesized relationships by means of regression analysis.

Econometric models vary considerably in their degree of sophistication. There are some models such as Bell's (1967) that have as few as 16 equations, while Glickman's Philadelphia IV model has 228 equations. The more elementary ones adopt the expenditure framework of economic base models given by equation (1.1) and are recursive in structure. In a recursive model, the equations can be ordered in such a way that there is a unidirectional flow of causality among sectors. For example,

$$X = a_o + a_1 \overline{GNP}$$
$$G = b_o + b_1 \overline{POP}$$
$$I = c_o + c_1 X$$
$$C = d_o + d_1 Y_d$$
$$M = e_1 Y_d$$
$$Y_d = (1 - t)Y$$
$$Y = f_o + f_1 \overline{GNP} \tag{1.12}$$

where GNP is Gross National Product and POP is population. Bars above the variables indicate that they are exogenous.

Here, the income, export, and government equations depend on exogenous variables. From there the flow of causation runs from income to disposable income to consumption and imports and, finally, to investment. In their most elementary form, econometric models emphasize external factors inducing growth or decline in a region and are thus quite similar to an economic base framework. They are demand oriented and treat wages and prices as given.

More sophisticated econometric models consider both internal and external sources of growth. Prices and wages for the region are determined within the system of equations postulated, and thus factor movement, in a neo-classical framework, can also be a consequence of exogenous shocks to the system. One factor emphasized in these models is labor supply, and equations explaining labor force and migration are critical elements.[12] Consumption, government and investment are specified by source (e.g., household, state and local, etc.) and thus considerably more detail is provided.

These more complex models stress the interdependence of the economic agents that compose the regional economy, and typically represent this interdependence by a simultaneous equation system. That is, each endogenous variable is determined at least partially by other endogenous variables. A typical equation would be:

$$V_i = V_i(V_j, Z) \tag{1.13}$$

where V's represent endogenous variables and Z's are exogenous variables.

Econometric models of the more complex variety are generally longer-run representations of the economy (with a time horizon of up to five years). They can incorporate aspects of changed structure such as productivity change, demographic composition, and industrial composition, and thus provide sources for growth that are absent in the other models. While the vast majority of econometric models are static, some attempts have been made to incorporate elements of dynamics into the model. Unlike the deterministic economic base models, econometric models attempt to empirically verify the theory upon which they are based.

1.3.2 Conceptual Problems

Given the great diversity in the construction of econometric models and the lack of a specific theory of regional growth to form a basis for the structure of these models, it is difficult to identify a general body of conceptual problems common to these undertakings.

In order to get additional perspective on some conceptual problems attached to regional econometric models, let us describe a representative framework of an econometric model. The regional economy is described by a series of behavioral relations that identify the major influence on output, employment, and income. These behavioral relations are related to the aggregate measures of performance by a social accounting system, much like the income accounts at the national level. For the nation, the income accounts are based upon a triple entry system which is given by the identity:

$$\text{GNP} = C + I + G + (X - M) = \text{NI} + D + \text{IBT}. \qquad (1.14)$$

That is, gross national product equals expenditures on consumption, investment, government, and exports minus imports, equals national income plus depreciation plus indirect business taxes. For a regional model, the expenditures approach cannot be implemented due to a lack of data. The income approach is also fraught with difficulties since information on depreciation and indirect business taxes is not available by region. Further, the only income data available is on income originating rather than income received, the latter being consistent with the national income concept. The output-income approach is typically used in regional models; however, there is no reason for these accounts to balance since, in the open regional economy, income originating does not equal income received. To use this accounting system, an approach such as Kendrick-Jaycox (1965) must be applied to generate missing elements in the accounts. Nevertheless, the accounting system which forms the framework for the model is incomplete.

In matrix form a simultaneous econometric model can be represented as:[13]

$$By_t + Cz_t = U_t$$

where

- B is a nonsingular matrix of coefficients of the endogenous variables $(G \times G)$
- y_t is a vector of G endogenous variables in period t
- C is a matrix of coefficients of the exogenous variables $(G \times K)$
- z_t is a vector of K exogenous variables (including lagged endogenous variables) in period t
- U_t is a vector of G random error terms in period t

If the structural model is linear in both parameters and variables, then the reduced form, used to predict the impact of exogenous changes on regional output, employment, and income, can be given by:

$$y_t = \pi z_t + v_t$$

where

$$\pi = -B^{-1}C \text{ and } v_t = B^{-1}U_t.$$

In the more realistic case, when there are nonlinearities in the variables, the structural form has to be "solved" by some numerical technique to obtain the endogenous in terms of the predetermined variables.

Regional econometric models are often highly linked to national models. Even though this linking has the benefit of easily providing forecasts of the exogenous variables, strict dependence on national variables influences the internal structure of the model. In some cases, this reduces regional analysis to determining regional income elasticity and industry mix.

Although the unique situation of each area studied is frequently incorporated in the model, little has been included in the way of specifically regional characteristics. While the economic problem of space is stressed in theoretical models of regional and urban economies, it is notably ignored in modeling these processes. Other omissions include intraregional resource allocation, import substitution, and regional capital markets. While constraints on data availability are partly responsible for this situation it does not fully explain this oversight.

Econometric models that incorporate investment and migration into the income-expenditure framework are capable of producing dynamic multipliers. As such they can show the cumulative impact of an exogenous shock over a number of years. Of the three models discussed, only econometric models are useful for longrun forecasting as well as for providing shortrun predictions of impact. The reliability of longrun impact studies is determined to a considerable extent by the availability of data on local investment and interregional migration.

1.3.3 Technical Problems

While the use of time series data is an important contribution of econometric models, a word of caution should be introduced in evaluating them. Because annual observations are generally the only data available for estimating the relationships of the model, flexibility in the choice of functional form is often severely limited. The more complex the specification, that is, the greater the number of endogenous and exogenous variables determining the variable of interest, the greater will be the number of observations required to realize an acceptable degree of statistical precision. The further back in time we go, the more likely it is that the underlying structure of the economy has changed so that simple linear or log-linear specifications may lead to severely biased parameter estimates. In this instance, more parsimonious structures or single-period models like the economic base may yield more accurate predictions than complex econometric models. Instead of reviewing these models and assessing their accuracy and degree of error, most researchers adopt a "love-'em and leave-'em" approach and do not provide an error analysis of their models.[14]

Data constraints also result in fewer explanatory variables being included in the equations than theory would suggest, or in incomplete specification of the regional system. Omission of these variables results in specification error that leads to statistically biased results. Where data problems have resulted in the construction of economic series, obvious biases in the coefficient of determination result. Ratajczak (1974) demonstrates that the relative lack of data need not severely compromise the specification. With specific techniques like the Kendrick-Jaycox method, assumptions such as identical regional production functions become incorporated in the model.

Econometric models, like economic base models, are generally highly static. The behavioral relationships tend to omit lagged variables since autocorrelation problems may result and relatively few degrees of freedom characterize the model.[15] Other statistical problems, such as multicollinearity, may bias coefficient estimates, and the interdependencies that exist in a region practically assure correlated movement of economic series.[16]

If sufficient data is available to construct a quarterly model, the resulting increased number of observations allows much more flexibility in specification. For example, the model can be made dynamic by including a variety of lag structures. This, in turn, allows investigation of disequilibrium phenomena and adjustment paths. Also, the increased number of degrees of freedom usually results in increased statistical precision of the estimated parameters.

There are also numerous problems encountered in trying to estimate the system of equations. While statistical tests are often employed in determining the structure of individual equations, a series of equations that are the "best fit" to the data in each equation will not necessarily yield the most accurate predictive model. While the process of equation aggregation is an important feature of econometric models, few researchers analyze this process.

1.3.4 Implementation

Econometric models offer many advantages over economic base models — they are more appropriate for longer-run problems and are capable of providing a great deal more detail. Behavioral relationships are estimated with time-series data by regression analysis so that underlying trends can be examined and hypotheses tested. These features are available at additional cost, however. In the case of the more simple econometric models, the basic core of equations is rather standardized and highly linked to national models. While there is room for modification to accommodate distinct features of the region, the basic framework for the model as well as a procedure for estimating the equations is available from an examination of previously published models. The level of expertise required to implement the model is considerably higher than that of the economic base model and there is substantially more data needed (although both the expertise and the data required are less than for a survey-based input-output model). As a consequence, the time needed to construct the model and the cost of doing so are substantially higher than for the base model.

1.4 INPUT-OUTPUT MODELS

1.4.1 Description

Input-output models provide a great deal of detail on the economic transactions that take place within a local economy and offer some understanding as to how impacts originating in one sector are transmitted throughout the economy.

In an input-output model each industry in the local economy is dependent upon every other industry. Sales by firms are dichotomized into intermediate and final uses. Production functions for each industry are linear and homogeneous so that economies and diseconomies of scale are disallowed and inputs must be used in fixed proportions. Prices and wages are assumed constant and no supply constraints exist. With these assumptions we can represent a typical input-output structure mathematically as:

$$\sum_{j=1}^{s} X_{ij} + \sum_{f=1}^{t} Y_{if} + e_i = X_i \qquad (i = 1, 2, \ldots, s) \qquad (1.15)$$

where

X_{ij} = sales of regional industry i to regional industry j
Y_{if} = sales of regional industry i to regional final demand sector f
e_i = export sales of regional industry i
X_i = total sales of regional industry i
s = number of industries
t = number of final-demand sectors excluding exports

The input side of the model is represented by

$$\sum_{i=1}^{s} X_{ij} + \sum_{p=1}^{t} V_{pj} + m_j = X_j \qquad (j = 1, \ldots, s) \qquad (1.16)$$

with

X_j = total production in industry j
V_{pj} = value-added by final payment sector p in industry j
m_j = imports by industry j

Since fixed coefficient production functions are assumed, each input must be purchased in fixed proportions to other inputs in order to produce a unit of output. The coefficient specifying the amount of input i needed to produce a unit of j is denoted a_{ij} and is derived by

$$a_{ij} = \frac{X_{ij}}{X_j} \qquad (1.17)$$

Substituting equation (1.17) into equation (1.16), we can represent the input-output system in matrix notation as:

$$AX + Y + E = X \qquad (1.18)$$

where the elements of the Y vector are

$$Y_i = \sum_{f=1}^{t} Y_{if}.$$

Solving this system for X we have

$$B(Y + E) = X \qquad (1.19)$$

where B equals $(I - A)^{-1}$, and b_{ij}, an element of the B matrix, represents the direct and indirect purchases of industry i from industry j in order to produce an additional unit of final demand.

Derivation of the multipliers is a rather straightforward exercise within this framework. A change in export demand (E^*) would lead to a total output change of BE^*. Income changes can be derived by multiplying the b_{ij} by coefficients representing value-added per unit of output, that is

$$k_j = \sum_i b_{ij} \cdot V_i \qquad (1.20)$$

where k_j is the multiplier and V_j is value added per unit of output in industry i. Employment multipliers can be derived by substituting employment for value-added in equation (1.20).

Frequently, the household final demand vector will be included in the technical matrix A to show the additional impact of changed incomes on final outputs. When this augmented matrix is used, elements of the corresponding inverse B^* represent the direct, indirect, and induced purchases of i from j required to satisfy one additional unit of final demand.

Because of the assumptions used to develop the input-output model, these models are only appropriate for analyzing shortrun problems. As the time horizon expands, the possibility of input substitution, technological change, etc., would require a revision of the input-output structure and a reestimation of the technical coefficients.

1.4.2 Conceptual Problems

The major conceptual problems of this model stem from the assumptions upon which the structure of the model is derived.

Growth or economic impact analysis is modeled by linear production functions for each industry. Any changes that are introduced in the system must consequently cause an equiproportionate increase or decrease in existing levels of resource use. Linearity also implies the absence of scale economies, which runs counter to important theoretical arguments for the existence of cities — namely agglomeration and urbanization economies.

Technical coefficients of the interindustry transactions matrix are assumed to be constant, thus making it difficult for technological change and productivity adjustments to be represented in the system. If these coefficients are taken to be the ratio of the value of transactions to total output then relative prices and wages must be assumed constant, or changes in trading patterns (substitution among inputs) will result in changed coefficients.

The models are usually static since dynamic features are difficult to incorporate in the model. Complex behavioral relationships governing capital formation by businesses and housing purchases by consumers are typically calculated outside of the model and forecasted values introduced as exogenous components of final demand. The exogenous components may then be included as part of an impact analysis by incorporating these final-demand columns into the interindustry transactions matrix and taking the inverse of the augmented matrix.

Change in regional structure, such as the introduction of a new industry, also presents a problem in the input-output model. It is the equivalent of adding a row and a column to the input-output table and recalculating a number of new coefficients. If the new industry is introduced sometime after the estimation of the table then there may be serious difficulties in updating the other coefficients without a new survey. Schaffer (1978) discusses this issue in the context of non-survey models.

1.4.3 Technical Problems

There are two distinct approaches to regional input-output models, and consequently two sets of technical problems: input-output tables may be constructed by census or survey methods, or by "borrowing" coefficients from other input-output tables.

If a survey rather than a full census is to be undertaken, the first problem encountered is that of sampling.[17] The sampling problem is how to determine the total number of firms and the number of firms per industry to be sampled. Many researchers either sample the largest employers until the budget is exhausted or simply take a random sample of all firms. If the task is to estimate industry production functions then the intraindustry variance in the proporation of inputs used should be the basis for sampling. For example, if all the firms in industry A have identical production functions, while the firms in industry B exhibit quite a bit of variance in the amounts of inputs used, then in order to minimize the total variation in the estimated production functions, we would want to sample more firms in B than in A.[18]

Once the sample is obtained, firms must somehow be aggregated into industries and their current purchases distinguished from investment. If there is a great deal of diversity among firms that produce similar products, or if there exist many multiproduct firms, the problem of aggregating firms into industries may be considerable. If one views each firm as an industry then the advantage of a model in assembling and collecting data into more meaningful categories is lost. On the other hand, too much aggregation will result in estimated production functions that have little correspondence with the economy that they are supposed to describe, as well as in producing biased forecasts. The aggregation process is dependent to a large extent on the researcher's judgment, and few studies speculate on the errors that might be introduced by their aggregation scheme.

In a survey approach, firms are requested to list the materials purchased for production. A plant manager or executive officer will frequently list purchases from the capital account in completing the response. It is then up to the researcher to carefully separate current from investment purchases. To the extent that the two accounts overlap, biases will be introduced into the model.

Finally, after assembling the data the input-output table must balance. That is, sales must equal purchases if the table is to have any validity. An input-output table based upon a sample will generally not balance after the initial effort. The reconciliation process (the process of equating "rows only" and "columns only" coefficients) is not based upon any generally accepted procedures. Individual judgment, often in conjunction with industry experts, is the basis for the reconciliation. What this implies is that two researchers with exactly the same data may construct two different input-output tables, and no information is available as to whether these differences would be nonmarginal.

Input-output tables constructed from sample data are very costly and cannot be completed quickly. On the other hand, considerable detail is supplied, and in certain situations a researcher has few options but to construct a table by sampling.

There are nonsurvey techniques available that are based upon adjusting technical coefficients from other input-output studies. Location quotients using employment or value-added may serve as the basis for the adjustment and therefore are subject to much the same criticism given above for the economic base model. After the technical coefficients have been adjusted to reflect local conditions, a regional purchase column must be calculated to show the percentage of sales of each industry that goes to local consumers. Often this column will be derived from either a limited survey or the judgment of experts. It appears that nonsurvey input-output models are quite similar to economic base models since they relate local to national (or regional) production techniques and thus are open to many of the same criticisms. As an input-output model, the additional criticisms raised earlier would be applicable.

In sum, the input-output model is most appropriate for shortrun forecasting problems where considerable detail is required. It does not seem to be appropriate for small local economies where interindustry relations are not important. This detail is obtained at a significant cost in the case of survey-based models. As far as aggregate estimation is concerned, a number of studies have shown the mathematical identity of input-output and economic base multipliers.[19] In practice, the aggregate multipliers derived from these two models tend to be similar.[20]

1.4.4 Implementation

Of the three models discussed, the input-output model presents the most difficulty for implementation. A survey-based model requires a vast amount of primary data and therefore involves considerable delay and expense. An input-output model for a small region could cost $250,000 and take two years to complete. The time and money costs are not the only impediments to undertaking a survey-based model. There are a substantial number of technical problems, such as appropriate definitions of capital and current expenses, that arise when an input-output model is constructed. Established procedures for estimating the technical coefficients are similarly unavailable and, consequently, a great deal of trial and error is involved. All of this is to point out that a great deal of expertise is vital to the construction of the model.

Nonsurvey-based input-output models, while measurably less expensive than survey models, also have a number of drawbacks. While there have been a number of procedures recommended for indirectly estimating the technical coefficients, little justification exists for selecting one procedure over another or over randomly selecting coefficients. In fact, Stevens and Trainer (1976) present some rather strong evidence that multipliers based upon the technical coefficient matrix are not very sensitive to randomly generated errors. Their research may have important implications for the appropriate methodology to be used in nonsurvey-based input-output models.

1.5 CONCLUSION

The multipliers derived from economic base, econometric, and input-output studies have been the subject of many evaluations. These numbers are evaluated against one another and frequently against some numbers that are believed to be the "true" values for a region but which actually are based on little more than intuition. In trying to evaluate the evaluations a word of caution needs to be introduced — there is no one method that yields generally superior multipliers. Some models, as we have tried to point out, are more appropriate for some problems than others. Many of the comparisons that are offered are made without regard to the problem at hand.

If an exogenous shock were introduced into a community and we wished to assess its impact after one year, one method would be to take a census prior to the announcement of the project and again one year after its completion. We could then total the employment, output, and income changes and compare these numbers with those predicted from the three models. However, even under these supposed ideal conditions one should not assume that the census will yield the "true" multiplier. A number of industries, such as the utilities, assess their labor needs on the basis of forecasted output. If these forecasts are not realized, the firms will reduce their employment. Even if the particular shock were not known or forecasted, as long as the increased demand falls within the forecasted increase in capacity, no new employment will result. Our models would predict an increase in employment based on historic output/employment ratios, and they would be more accurate than the survey that did not count the employment increase. The survey team would also have to be careful that all other exogenous factors were accounted for. This is easy to do in a model but more difficult to do in the real world. It is therefore difficult to evaluate which of the three models yields "better" multipliers without additional information as to the intended application. Even a survey might yield incorrect assessments if the information is not requested and interpreted correctly.

Frequently, economic base multipliers will be compared with input-output multipliers where the latter are regarded as true values. As we have seen, input-output models have a number of conceptual and technical problems (as do economic base models), so that we do not know which of the two is closer to the true value. Secondly, input-output models are usually developed for larger areas like states, and the larger the area to be considered, the further is the estimated economic base model from its theoretical construct.

The most damaging evidence against an economic base model based upon minimum requirements or location quotients stems from a study by David Greytak (1969). Comparing estimation error associated with location quotients and minimum requirements with special survey data on regional exports, Greytak found that both techniques were subject to considerable systematic error. With the level of aggregation selected by Greytak, location quotients had larger error than exhibited by minimum requirements. In defense of these techniques, it should be pointed out that Greytak's choice of an aggregation level did not present the most favorable case for either technique. Location quotients and, hence, the multiplier, increase in accuracy as disaggregation occurs, whereas the opposite is true for minimum requirements. Since highly aggregated data for location quotients were the basis for the comparison, Greytak's conclusions must be treated with a bit of skepticism.

The local economy which all three models attempt to describe is dynamic and probably in a state of constant disequilibrium. All models implicitly assume that at the reference point (or points) the economy is in equilibrium. Further, all models are highly static so that the dynamic relationships inherent in the economy are not well represented. Does this criticism imply that the models are not very accurate in forecasting change? No, it merely means that too much should not be expected of these models and that accuracy should be defined in relative terms. If one wished to know the time of day, there would be a number of alternatives available, such as a watch, a sundial, a clock, etc. It would be extremely unlikely that any of these estimates of the time would be exact, but, depending upon the particular situation, any or none of these estimates may be acceptable.

That the economy is in a state of disequilibrium does not disturb the models as long as the disequilibrium situation remains constant. In mathematical terms one could include a slack variable in any market clearing equation. The importance of including dynamics increases with the length of the forecast period and the particular models being employed. For short-run forecasting (less than five years) a static approximation should not lead to important biases. Forecasts for more than a five-year time horizon may cause problems, especially with the economic base and input-output models.

This overview has tried to summarize the characteristics of three basic types of regional models that have been and are being used for economic impact analysis. If there is to be an optimizing approach to the selection of a model, it is important to understand the conceptual and technical problems inherent in each model. Recognition of these limitations will tend to reduce one type of error. The other ingredient to an impact analysis, a forecast of the exogenous variable(s), has been virtually ignored in this review. This is not to diminish the impact that forecast errors have on the analysis. In fact, if forecast error can be reduced with additional expenditures, there should be a trade-off between expenditures on modeling efforts and expenditures on forecasting exogenous variables. As Stevens and Trainer (1976) show, expenditures on the latter may even have a higher pay-off.

NOTES

1. The term *indirect effects* is used in a very general sense and includes induced effects where appropriate.
2. See, for example, Hildebrand and Mace (1950), Mathur and Rosen (1974), and Park (1970).
3. S. Gerking (1976).
4. Treyz, Friedlander, and Stevens (1978), Chalmers (1978).
5. See D. Garnick (1969) and Tiebout (1962) for examples of disaggregated economic base models, Bell (1967) and Glickman (1971) for examples of aggregated econometric models.
6. The economic base model has a considerable history starting with Robert Haig (1926). For a rather complete bibliography of the early work on the economic base model, see Isard (1960), pp. 227–231.
7. See Charles M. Tiebout (1962) for a more detailed description of these models.
8. See Weiss and Gooding (1968) and Hildebrand and Mace (1950).
9. If firm A sells a product to firm B, the output price of firm B includes the price of firm A so that counting sales leads to the double counting of A values.

10. The description to follow uses employment as the unit of measurement. Any of the other variables mentioned previously could have been used with the same difficulties noted above.
11. See Pindyck and Rubinfeld (1976).
12. See for example, Henry Fishkind (1977) and Norman Glickman (1974).
13. The notation presented here is from Glickman (1977).
14. For the importance of error analysis, see Fishkind (1977).
15. Autocorrelation occurs when the error terms in a regression equation are not independent over time. If a large error in year $t - 1$ influences the size of the error in year t, then biased estimates of sample variances will result.
16. When multicollinearity is present it is difficult to separate the independent influence of the explanatory variables in determining the variable of interest.
17. For a complete description of the sampling problem, see Gerking and Pleeter (1978).
18. In fact, if all firms in A had identical production functions, we would only need to sample one firm.
19. See R. Billings (1969).
20. For some comparisons, see R. Webster et al. (1976).

2 ALTERNATIVE ECONOMIC BASE BIFURCATION TECHNIQUES: THEORY, IMPLEMENTATION, AND RESULTS

Andrew Isserman*

2.1 INTRODUCTION

The economic base model divides a region's economic activity into two sectors: a basic sector that satisfies demand originating outside the region, and a nonbasic sector that satisfies internal demand. In order to use the economic base model for impact analysis or forecasting, it is therefore necessary to estimate the levels of basic and nonbasic activity; that is to bifurcate total activity. However, no single method of bifurcation has gained universal acceptance. Four main techniques exist in the literature. Each has its own advocates who usually serve as critics of the other techniques. Because of the central role of these techniques in estimating impact multipliers, a detailed analysis of their theoretical rationales, data requirements, and empirical properties seems to be warranted. Such an analysis is presented here, as are procedural recommendations and a comparison of estimates for cities in the United States.[1]

To a large extent this paper is a reexamination of previous work. However, it is hoped when undertaking such a review that the juxtaposition of

*Associate Professor of Urban and Regional Planning and Economics, University of Illinois.

research efforts formerly spread over time and space results in new perspective, understanding, and in the discovery of numerous loose ends and misinterpretations.

2.2 THE ECONOMIC BASE MODEL

In the simplest and most widely applied form of the model, nonbasic activity is assumed to depend on and be proportional to basic activity. The basic sector is considered the "basis" of the region's growth, because any change in basic activity causes a change in nonbasic activity sufficient to restore their previous proportional relationship. Algebraically, letting E represent total economic activity, X basic activity, N nonbasic activity, and r the region,

$$E_r = X_r + N_r \tag{2.1}$$

$$N_r = pX_r \tag{2.2}$$

and, therefore,

$$E_r = (1 + p)X_r \tag{2.3}$$

The term $(1 + p)$ is the impact multiplier relating changes in total activity to changes in basic activity. As can be seen from equation (2.3), the multiplier can be calculated by dividing basic activity into total activity.

The economic base model can be formulated without assuming the fixed proportional relationship between basic and nonbasic activity of equation (2.2). For example, assuming

$$N_r = a + bX_r \tag{2.4}$$

and substituting into Equation 1,

$$E_r = a + (1 + b)X_r. \tag{2.5}$$

In this more general case the impact multiplier $(1 + b)$ cannot be calculated just by dividing basic into total activity. The parameter b must be estimated using multiple observations. This need for additional data probably explains the great popularity of the more simple model embodying the proportionality assumption of equation (2.2).

Whatever the form of the functional relationship between nonbasic and basic activity, it is necessary to bifurcate the economy. The four techniques to be discussed do so in very different ways. The next sections discuss the procedures and theoretical rationales of each technique in turn.

2.2.1 Modified Location Quotient Approach

The location quotient is a measure of relative concentration and can be expressed as follows:

$$\mathrm{LQ}_{ir} = \frac{E_{ir}/E_r}{E_{in}/E_n} = \frac{E_{ir}/E_{in}}{E_r/E_n} \tag{2.6}$$

where the subscript i indicates a specific industry, n indicates the nation or another area, and r indicates the region under study.

Basic employment, that is, employment producing for external demand, can be estimated by

$$X_{ir} = (1 - 1/\mathrm{LQ}_{ir})E_{ir} \qquad \text{if } \mathrm{LQ}_{ir} > 1, \tag{2.7}$$

this is equal to

$$X_{ir} = \left(\frac{E_{ir}}{E_{in}} - \frac{E_r}{E_n} \right) E_{in}. \tag{2.8}$$

This last formulation is most useful for understanding the theoretical rationale behind the location quotient approach. The first term, which is the region's share of the nation's employment in industry i, is a proxy for its share of production if productivity per employee is identical in the region and the nation. The second term, which is the region's share of the nation's total employment, is a proxy for its share of consumption if consumption of good i per employee is identical in the region and the nation.[2]

When the production share is greater than the consumption share, the excess is assumed to be produced for external demand and constitutes basic activity in industry i. Illustrating with a simple example, if a region has 7 percent of the nation's employment in industry i and 4 percent of the nation's total employment, under the location quotient approach, it is assumed that the difference between those amounts, or 3 percent of the nation's employment in industry i, is producing to satisfy demand originating outside the region.

The use of equation (2.8) in estimating basic activity involves two assumptions in addition to the equal average productivity and consumption assumptions. It is assumed implicitly that the region's consumption of i comes entirely from the region's production. However, if, in fact, three-quarters of the region's consumption of i consists of imports, and only one-quarter consists of locally produced goods, then surplus production for external demand would actually be 6 percent, that is, $7 - (\frac{1}{4}) 4$. In short, to the extent that the region imports good i, the location quotient approach underestimates basic activity.

This discussion is related to the difference between gross and net basic activity. Gross basic activity is the relevant measure for use in calculating economic base multipliers; it is a measure of the amount of production for external demand. Net basic activity is that amount minus the amount imported to serve internal demand. Because total regional consumption is being subtracted from production in equation (2.8), and because total consumption includes both consumption from the region's production and consumption of imports, the result is a measure of net basic activity, although gross basic is needed. This potential dilemma is typically resolved by assuming that there are no imports of goods which are exported, that is, no crosshauling. Then gross and net are equal, and the location quotient is measuring the right thing. However, since crosshauling does exist, because of brand preferences and heterogenous products being grouped under each industry, the location quotient does estimate net basic, and, therefore, underestimates gross basic activity.

The final assumption underlying equation (2.8) is that the nation is not a net exporter or importer of good i. Since, from the second assumption, 4 percent of the nation's employees consumed 4 percent of its production, the entire nation must consume an amount equal to its entire production. The nation may export and import good i, but under equation (2.8) its *net* exports of good i are assumed to be zero.

In light of the four assumptions, the location quotient technique is a crude estimator of exogenous employment (but, as will be seen, so are its competitors). Two procedural steps are essential in improving its accuracy. The technique should be implemented using data at the most detailed level of disaggregation; and all federal government employment should be assigned to the exogenous sector, since federal jobs bring outside money into the region in the same manner as manufacturing jobs producing goods for exports. Further modification to relax the four assumptions, by incorporating productivity and consumption variations and recognizing national net exports, are discussed in Isserman (1977a) (from which much of this section was drawn).

2.2.2 Minimum Requirements Approach

This approach was pioneered by Ullman and Dacey (1960). Its main difference from the location quotient approach is that the region's employment structure is compared to a sample of similar-sized regions rather than to the nation as a whole. For each industry i, the region within each size class that has the minimum share of its employment devoted to i is identified. Every other region within the size class is assumed to produce for external demand, with the basic sector consisting of the difference between an industry's share of employment in the region and that industry's share in the region where it attains its minimum value. In equation form:

$$X_{ir} = \left(\frac{E_{ir}}{E_r} - \frac{E_{im}}{E_m} \right) E_r \tag{2.9}$$

where m stands for the region in r's size class that has the smallest value for E_{im}/E_m.[3]

Equation (2.8), the location quotient equation, can be rearranged to more effectively contrast the two approaches:

$$X_{ir} = \left(\frac{E_{ir}}{E_r} - \frac{E_{in}}{E_n} \right) E_r. \tag{2.10}$$

Thus, whereas the location quotient approach assigns to basic all employment greater than the national average share of the economy (E_{in}/E_n), the minimum requirement approach assigns all employment greater than the group minimum (E_{im}/E_m).

This rather small structural difference between the two approaches does have significant implications for the underlying assumptions, as can be seen by rearranging equation (2.9), the minimum requirements equation:

$$\left(\frac{E_{ir}}{E_{in}} - \frac{E_{im}}{E_{in}} \frac{E_r}{E_m} \right) E_{in}. \tag{2.11}$$

Following the same procedure as with equation (2.8) for the location quotient approach, the first term in the parentheses is a proxy for the region's production if the equal productivity assumption is made. However, the consumption term is a bit more complex. It is assumed that the region's consumption, expressed as a fraction of the nation's production, is equal to the minimum region's fraction scaled by the relative size of total employment in the minimum region and the region under study (E_r/E_m). In other words, the region is assumed to consume the same amount per employee as does the minimum region. Thus, the equal consumption assumption is made relative to the minimum region rather than to the national average.

The "no crosshauling" assumption is implicit in the minimum requirements procedure just as it was in the location quotient procedure. Every region, except the one which has the minimum share for industry i, is assumed to produce for export; and the minimum region is assumed to take care of its own consumption. As Pratt (1968) observed, "The technique presents a paradox in that it leads to a group of cities in which each city exports and none imports. . . . The theory clearly precludes the importing of any goods or services for internal consumption" (pp. 118–119). There is no importing and no crosshauling, just as in the location quotient approach, because every region is assumed to produce at least enough to satisfy its own consumption.

However, there is an alternative interpretation of the consumption term. It can be considered to be an estimate, not of total regional consumption of *i*, but of regional consumption *from the region's production*. In that case, since total regional consumption consists of consumption from the region's production plus consumption of imports, regions can both import and export, and crosshauling can exist. The minimum requirement approach, when interpreted this way, estimates gross exports. Pratt's paradox disappears, as even (and particularly) the minimum region imports to augment its consumption from local production.

In sum, then, the minimum requirement technique attempts to measure the fraction of a region's production which goes to satisfy local demand. Whereas the location quotient approach measures the region's total consumption, the minimum requirement approach tries to predict what part of local consumption is produced locally.[4] However, there is no compelling reason for assuming that the minimum actually is that sought-after number. For example, the minimum region itself may be an exporter, so that its entire production is not for local consumption, as assumed by the minimum requirement approach. Thus, the first possibility for error is that the minimum region is not a "pure" nonexporter. The second possibility for error is that, even if it is a complete nonexporter, other regions may have larger or smaller shares of their employment producing for local consumption. There is no convincing theoretical argument that all cities in a size group should devote the same share of their labor force to production for internal demand.

The location quotient has an excellent theoretical rationale as a measure for net basic activity, but is being used in the economic base model as a proxy for gross basic activity. On the other hand, the minimum requirement may seek to measure the right thing (consumption from local production), but the number it uses, the minimum share, has no strongly compelling rationale. All that can be said in its favor is that, like the true number, the minimum share is lower than the average consumption used in the location quotient approach. It may generate a better estimate, unless it is too low. That possibility is discussed later in this paper.

2.2.3 Assignment Approach

This procedure has no underlying theoretical rationale. Employment in each industry is assigned to basic or nonbasic according to the analyst's judgment. Sometimes the assignments are the end result of a careful survey of the region's main employers, but usually industries are assigned entirely to one or the other sector. In that case it is hoped that the overestimates of basic activity in the industries assigned entirely to basic are balanced by the underestimates of basic activity in the industries assigned entirely to nonbasic. Commonly, agriculture, mining, manufacturing, and federal government are assigned to the basic sector and all other industries to nonbasic, but there are variations; for example, see Field and Convery (1976), Garnick (1970), and Polzin (1973). An obvious modification of the technique, which has been adopted by some analysts, is to assign parts of industries to each sector.

2.2.4 Mathur-Rosen Approach

An econometric approach has been recommended by Mathur and Rosen (Mathur and Rosen, 1974; Rosen and Mathur, 1973). It estimates the fraction of employment in i which is exogenous by ordinary least-squares regression, using time series data in the form:

$$E_{ir} = \alpha + \beta E_n + \Sigma \tag{2.13}$$

or

$$\ln E_{ir} = \alpha + \beta E_n + \Sigma \tag{2.14}$$

Substituting mean values of E_{ir} and E_n into the regression equation causes the error term to drop out. Then both sides of the equation are divided by E_{ir}, yielding, in the case of equation (2.13),

$$1 = \frac{\alpha}{\bar{E}_{ir}} + \frac{\beta \bar{E}_n}{\bar{E}_{ir}}. \tag{2.13a}$$

Mathur and Rosen hypothesize that "the proportion of ith industry's employment in r which is sensitive to total employment in the rest of the world (E_n) is nonlocalized (basic), while the directly insensitive portion is localized" (1974, p. 93). Thus, the second term on the left in equation (2.14) estimates the fraction of the industry's employment which is basic, whereas the first term is the nonbasic fraction.

There are a number of problems with this technique. As noted in Isserman (1975 and 1977b), by assuming that all activity which is "sensitive" to national activity is basic, the approach ignores the key defining characteristic of the economic base model, namely that nonbasic activity depends on basic activity (equations (2.2) and (2.4)). The problem can be shown algebraically with a slight simplification of the method for expository purposes. The following set of equations repeats the economic base model and the bifurcation equation:

$$E_r = X_r + N_r \tag{2.15}$$

$$N_r = a + bX_r \tag{2.16}$$

$$X_r = cE_n. \tag{2.17}$$

Substituting into equation (2.15) results in

$$E_r = a + (1 + b)cE_n. \tag{2.18}$$

Equation (2.18) is a simplified version of equation (2.13) expressed in terms of the economic base model variables. Plugging in average values for E_r and E_n leads to

$$1 = \frac{a}{E_r} + \frac{(1 + b)cE_n}{E_r}. \tag{2.19}$$

The term on the far right is analogous to Mathur's and Rosen's "employment in r which is sensitive to employment in the rest of the world"; it is their estimate of the basic share. Yet note its structure: from equation (2.17), X_r/E_r should be equal to cE_n/E_r. Instead, this technique has assigned to basic activity not only basic activity as estimated by equation (2.17), but also that activity's impact on nonbasic activity (bcE_n). What is left to the nonbasic sector is simply the exogenous part of nonbasic activity (a). In other words, because "this estimate of basic employment also includes the non-basic employment which indirectly varies with world employment," through equations (2.16) and (2.17), "it is an overestimate of basic employment" (Isserman, 1975, p. 290).

The method has another problematic empirical property. Although the basic and nonbasic shares do sum to one, one or the other is often a negative number. Also, this method tends to assign employment on the basis of secular trends, sometimes in direct contradiction of a priori logic. Local government and services often are assigned to basic because of their recent relative growth; whereas federal military and agriculture tend to be assigned to nonbasic because their patterns in many areas have differed from that of national employment, for instance, decreasing while national employment increases, and therefore resulting in a negative basic share. Finally, the approach is most inappropriate for areas that are not linked tightly to national employment as the source of exogenous demand.

2.3 IMPLEMENTATION AND EMPIRICAL PROPERTIES

The location quotient approach requires the most data in terms of industrial detail. As noted earlier, its estimates become more plausible as the input data becomes more disaggregated. Table 2–1 shows the increase in the estimate of basic activity which accompanies the use of more disaggregated employment data. The largest changes occur in the first step of disaggregation, with an average increase of 109 percent in basic activity for the four areas shown.[5] Since data are often not available below the two-digit level in developing countries and, because of disclosure rules, for small regions in developed countries, successful use of the location quotient approach may be impeded in those settings.

Even with data on the four-digit SIC level, the location quotient approach probably underestimates gross basic activity because of crosshauling. However, failure of the other three assumptions underlying this approach (in certain directions) could counteract the effect of the failure of the crosshauling assumption.

Recall the assumption that the nation has no net exports of good i. If the nation being studied is, in fact, a net exporter, the estimate of basic activity in the region will be too low for yet another reason. According to equation (2.8), the region's share of the nation's employment is equal to its share of consumption of the nation's production. If there is net exporting, the nation is consuming less than its total production, and, therefore, less than

Table 2–1.   The effect of data dissaggregation on the basic share of economic activity as estimated by location quotients

Area	Division data	Two-digit data	Three-digit data	Four-digit data	Modified four-digit*
Georgia	.053	.152	.182	.207	.267
Kansas	.097	.154	.209	.233	.292
West Virginia	.120	.239	.287	.318	.347
Philadelphia	.058	.110	.166	.193	.253

*All federal government employment was added to the basic sector.
Source: Derived from data presented in Isserman (1977a).

the region's employment share should have been deducted from the region's production in estimating the region's exports. Thus the approach is particularly ill-suited for goods which are significant national exports, unless an adjustment is made to the consumption fraction (E_r/E_n) by multiplying it by the national export fraction. On the other hand, for goods that are imported nationally, violation of the no-net-import assumption counteracts the bias from the no crosshauling assumption. In fact, if the nation and the region are both net importers of the same fraction of their consumption of good i, the two "errors" of importing and crosshauling balance out. Indeed, the location quotient theoretically is more accurate in that situation than when the no-net-export or -import assumption holds.

The minimum requirements approach can be implemented using roughly division or one-digit level data for a sample of regions of similar size to the study region. With further disaggregation of the database more exogenous activity is identified, but Ullman asserts that the most realistic estimates are derived from the fourteen-sector breakdown used by the U.S. Census.

Ullman and Dacey added the minimum requirements by industry within each region size group to yield the local sector as a fraction of total employment. A regression was run with the local fraction as the dependent variable and logarithm of population as the independent variable. Moore (1975) replicated and updated the Ullman-Dacey study and derived the equation:

$$\frac{N_r}{E_r} = -20.36538 + 13.78340 \log \text{Pop.} \tag{2.20}$$

The equation enables the very rapid calculation of the local share and, thereby, the basic share of a region's employment. If the region is an SMSA or city in the U.S. (the unit used by Ullman and Dacey and Moore), equation (2.13) can be utilized rather than proceeding *de novo* to derive size group minima.[6]

An argument can be made that the minimum requirements approach, like the location quotient approach, underestimates basic activity. The region with the minimum share is assumed to produce entirely for its own consumption. At the level of aggregation recommended by Ullman and Dacey, e.g., durable goods manufacturing, this crucial premise is highly unlikely. In that case, with even the minimum share region producing for external demand, the minimum share overstates consumption from a region's production and thereby underestimates basic activity. On the other hand, it is quite plausible that a region with a relatively large share of, say, manufacturing employment not only exports more manufacturing products than a region with a smaller share, but probably also consumes more from its own production than the minimum region does. To the extent that regions do produce more for their own consumption than the minimum share indicates, the technique may not be underestimating basic activity after all. Borrowing the words from Ullman, Dacey, and Brodsky (1969, pp. 19–20), one might be tempted to conclude that the choice is between the irrelevant average of the location quotient and a false minimum. Moreover, it is unknown whether this "minimum" over- or understates the true value.

The assignment technique can be carried out with data at any level of aggregation. Presumably more detailed data would enable separating largely local subcategories from largely basic categories; for instance, dairy production from manufacturing, or gravel mining (for local construction) from mining. The assignment approach does not seem to be widely used by practitioners; its incorporation into more sophisticated techniques of analysis, however, has already been noted.

Yet the assignment approach does have more potential as a bifurcation technique. Given the propensity of the location quotient to underestimate basic employment, combining the assignment and location quotient approaches may be a pragmatic step in the direction of accuracy. For example, assigning most manufacturing subcategories to basic may be an appropriate strategy to counteract the location quotient's probable underestimation in other industries. Of course, the optimal extent of counteraction is not known.

The Mathur-Rosen approach to bifurcation requires time-series data for both the region and the nation (or other reference area). To date there has been little analysis of the effects of the level of aggregation of the data on the actual results. However, it can be assumed that this approach overestimates exports, as noted previously. This property, when combined with the location quotient, enables a bracketing approach, whereby upper and lower limits of basic activity are estimated (Isserman, 1975 and 1977b). However, in a preliminary, crude investigation the bounds (expressed in shares) turned out to be quite wide: .305 to .556 for the state of Kansas and .282 to .847 for the state of Washington (1977b, p. 1010). The accuracy of the econometric approach probably could be improved through judicious assignments, as was the case with the location quotient. For example, transferring services and local government to nonbasic might be justified in cases where their secular growth led to obviously unrealistic estimates.

A general choice among the four bifurcation approaches would be difficult, as well as unnecessary, to make at this point. Data availability may dictate the choice in an actual situation, but it is not surprising that after this review no one technique has completely dominated the others. Instead, the main impression well may be the disquieting, problematic nature of every approach. Each has its serious conceptual flaws: the irrelevant average, the false minimum, the arbitrary assignment, and the entangled econometric approach. But what difference does the choice of technique actually make? In the next section the comparison of these approaches continues by examining actual estimates of basic activity made by each technique.

2.4 EMPIRICAL EVALUATIONS

There are surprisingly few comparisons between the bifurcation estimates and survey-based data. Moreover, of the seven studies noted here, four focus entirely on manufacturing and only two examine more than one bifurcation technique. Leven (1956), in an important, comprehensive paper, compared the division-level distribution of basic activity in five Midwest metropolitan areas, as estimated by sample survey and location quotients. He found that the "differences are quite striking and are certainly not systematic" (pp. 257–258). However, his results say little about the key question here: how accurate is the estimate of total basic activity? It is the magnitude of basic activity, not its distribution among divisions, that is of interest.[7]

Ullman and Dacey (1960) report that minimum requirements estimated 56 percent basic activity for Sioux City, whereas Leven estimated 59 percent by survey. Similarly, they report convergence with other studies, 59 percent versus 56 percent (MR) for Madison and 37 percent "by both methods" in Oshkosh; for manufacturing alone, 96 versus 93 percent (MR) in Oshkosh and 92 versus 86 percent in South Bend. However, the methods used in the other studies are not noted, and Ullman-Dacey themselves recognize that these "few comparisons" are not "conclusive evidence of the correctness of the minimum requirements methods, because of limitation in number, different methods of classification and/or different dates, as well as possible error in the other estimates" (p. 189). In their follow-up study, Ullman, Dacey, and Brodsky (1969) compare minimum requirements to survey studies by Hansen, Robson, and Tiebout of the Los Angeles and San Francisco SMSAs. The estimates of total basic activity are 27 and 29 percent (MR) in Los Angeles and 28 and 34 percent (MR) in San Francisco. There is no comparison with location quotients.

Tiebout (1962) compared location quotient and survey estimates of the basic share of two-digit manufacturing industries in six cities — twenty-seven industry observations in all. The location quotient underestimated the survey every time with a mean location quotient estimate of 49 percent and a survey mean of 93 percent. However, the role of aggregation in the location quotient approach is important here. The estimate of total basic share increased by 45 percent on average when using four-digit rather than two-digit data (table 2–1). Increasing Tiebout's 49 percent mean estimate by that 45 percent reduces the gap between his location quotient and survey means to 71 versus 93 percent. Nevertheless, the location quotient approach still underestimates. In fact, for these manufacturing activities, as well as for the two Ullman and Dacey examples, the assignment approach to manufacturing seems to be a pragmatic strategy.

Leigh (1972) compared location quotient estimates to 1958 survey data for manufacturing exports from the Vancouver metropolitan area. He found that location quotients captured only 57 percent of the exports. However, using the data presented in his paper, the crucial role of disaggregation is illustrated again. The fifteen industries presented consist of eight two-digit industries and seven on the three- or four-digit level. For the first group only 4 percent of exports was identified; in the second group, 87 percent was!

Further evidence regarding the choice between the location quotient and assignment approaches can be gleaned by further processing of Leigh's data. Actual sales in the seven three- or four-digit industries were 28,040 (units not presented), surveyed exports were 17,055, and the location quotient estimate was 14,816. Thus the location quotient approach is far more accurate here than is the assignment approach, in contrast to the evidence in Tiebout (1962).

Greytak (1969) compared estimates for both the minimum requirement and the location quotient approaches to a special tabulation of data from the *1963 Census of Transportation*. His study is the most refined and comprehensive to date, but it is limited to data on manufacturing industries on the two-digit level for seven states or state groupings. (The minimum requirement is calculated using the seven units as a single-size group.) Greytak found average errors of 58.3 percent (MR) and 92.1 percent (LQ) of the mean of the actual values of gross exports by industry. However, as noted in Isserman (1977a), neither bifurcation approach was implemented at its preferred level of aggregation — division for minimum requirement (according to Ullman) and four-digit for location quotient. In the latter case Greytak's data imply that the result would have been more successful with more disaggregated data, because 75 percent of the error is an error of central tendency. In fact, after correction by a linear transformation, only an 8 percent error remained with the location quotient and a 20 percent error with minimum requirements. In short, for manufacturing at least, Greytak found that the location quotients erred systematically. However, no subsequent work has been done to see whether Greytak's linear transformation generalizes to other data sets, i.e., to determine an optimal adjustment strategy of the location quotient approach.

Isserman (1977b) proposed a method for processing existing regional input-output tables to generate estimates of the basic shares of a region's economic activity. These survey-based estimates then could be used as standards to measure the accuracy of the alternative bifurcation techniques. The sales coefficient technique for estimating the basic share presented in that paper can be shown to equal:

$$\frac{X_r}{E_r} = \frac{U'(I - A)^{-1}F_x}{U'Q} \tag{2.21}$$

where $(I - A)^{-1}$ is the Leontief matrix; U is a column vector all of whose elements are ones; F_x is a column vector of final demand from the basic sectors, e.g., export and federal government; and Q is a column vector of total output. In short, all production of intermediate goods needed to produce F_x is assigned to basic, while intermediate and final production related to the other final demand sectors is assigned implicitly to nonbasic.

However, there is a second, related strategy:

$$\frac{X_r}{E_r} = \frac{U'F_x}{U'Q}. \tag{2.22}$$

In equation (2.22) the economy is closed with respect to all but the basic final-demand sectors, which is more consistent with the economic base model. The difference between equations (2.21) and (2.22) is analogous to the difference between Type I (household exogenous) and Type II (household endogenous) input-output multipliers. The truth lies somewhere in between, as assumed by equation (2.5) of the economic base model, because nonbasic activity has both an endogenous and an exogenous component.

The Type I approach of Equation (2.21) found basic shares of .358 and .495 in Kansas and Washington respectively, whereas the location quotient estimated .305 and .282 and the Mathur-Rosen approach .556 and .847. Since the Type II benchmark would be lower than the Type I and the truth lies between them, the evaluation of the location quotient using this strategy remains inconclusive; but the Mathur-Rosen estimates are unambiguously too high, as argued in the last section. Research with the Type I and Type II estimates is continuing for more than 15 regions in hopes of generating more conclusive results.

In summary, empirical evaluations of the approaches remain incomplete and unconvincing. The location quotient probably does underestimate basic activity, as the limited empirical evidence, largely for manufacturing, is consistent with the theoretical expectation. The minimum requirement has been tested even less, but, importantly, although its errors are smaller than the location quotient's (for manufacturing exports), its errors are less systematic. Finally, the assignment approach has not been tested, but there is some fragmentary evidence supporting its use for manufacturing (as well as some evidence against its use). In the absence of conclusive theoretical or empirical evidence for any one approach, actual estimates of basic activity made by each approach are compared in the next section.

2.5 COMPARISON OF RESULTS

In doing the impact studies required of them by law, the U.S. Forest Service uses the assignment approach, the U.S. Army the location quotient, and the U.S. Air Force the minimum requirement. Rarely does an analyst explore the implications of his choice of bifurcation technique on the impact he or she is predicting. What difference does the choice of technique actually make? Are the variations great, or do all techniques produce similar estimates? Moreover, are the variations systematic, as Ullman, Dacey, and Brodsky (1969, p. 16) speculate ("measuring from the average (LQ) will practically always produce a smaller export than measuring from the minimum")?

To begin to answer these questions, the basic share of total wage and salary employment was estimated using the location quotient and minimum requirement approaches for a nonrandom sample of 101 standard metropolitan statistical areas (SMSAs) in the United States. These cities range in size from New York, with a 1972 estimated population of 11,565,000, to Cheyenne, Wyoming, with a population of 59,700. Then for 39 of these SMSAs in five groups (largest cities, federal centers, state capitals or universities, manufacturing cities, and sunbelt cities), the bifurcation was made by assignment as well.

Cities were chosen as the unit of analysis in order to use the convenient equation for minimum requirements calculated by Moore (1975) and previously presented in this paper as equation (2.20). Although Moore's and the earlier calibrations of that equation by Ullman and Dacey (1960) and Ullman, Dacey, and Brodsky (1969) included small cities of 2500 or more population, only SMSAs with more than 50,000 population are included here. There are two reasons for this decision. First, the detailed, industry-specific data needed to implement the location quotient approach correctly are not available below the county level. Since SMSAs are defined as either single counties or combinations of counties and were used by Moore to represent the large cities, SMSAs are the only units used in calibrating the minimum requirements equation for which a valid comparison of the approaches can be made. Second, an SMSA is an integrated economic region by definition and therefore a compelling unit for an economic base study, because there is no need to model intrametropolitan leakages caused by differences in location of working, living, and shopping places. As was the case in the minimum requirement studies, only "free-standing" or monocentered SMSAs were included. Thus, for example, the Hartford-New Britain-Bristol SMSA in Connecticut and the Salinas-Seaside-Monterey SMSA in California were omitted.

The location quotient bifurcation used the most detailed data available, generally four-digit-level data, with all federal employment and hotel and motel employment assigned to the basic sector. As mentioned before, despite those assignments, the location quotient approach is expected to underestimate the basic share because of its implicit assumption of no crosshauling and its net rather than gross property.

In contrast to the Ullman, Dacey, and Brodsky hypothesis, 22 of the 101 SMSAs had a greater estimate of the basic share with the location quotient approach than with minimum requirements. Thus in more than 20 percent of the cases, the minimum requirement yielded an estimate lower than a number considered to be too low. Although there are circumstances under which the location quotient may not underestimate basic activity, e.g., a region with low productivity and high consumption rates specializing in products which are exported nationally, it would appear to be reasonable generally to discard a minimum requirement estimate which is less than its location quotient counterpart. In addition, a modification of the minimum requirement approach is suggested whereby it is only applied to employment other than federal government, with the latter assigned entirely to basic activity, as was done with the location quotient.

The empirical properties of the alternative approaches can be examined more closely using the results presented in tables 2–2 through 2–6. Estimates using one of the infinite variations on the assignment approach are shown, too. Farming, federal and state government employment, manufacturing, and mining were assigned to basic activity. State government employment had to be estimated, because state and local government are combined in the data series provided by the Bureau of Economic Analysis. State employment for each SMSA was crudely estimated by using that state government's share of state and local government expenditure in 1971 as reported by the Advisory Commission on Inter-governmental Relations (ACIR) (1977).

The location quotient yielded a higher estimate of basic activity than minimum requirements for five of the ten largest SMSAs in the United States (table 2–2); and, in four of the remaining five, the estimates are within 10 percent of one another. Whereas the minimum requirement formula

Table 2-2.   Basic share of wage and salary employment, 1972, as estimated by alternative bifurcation techniques—ten largest SMSAs

SMSA	Pop. 1972 (1000's)[a]	LQ[b]	MR[c]	A[d]	Three largest sectors[e]		
New York	11565	.397	.230	.277	23%S,	20%T,	19%M
Chicago	7054	.280	.260	.382	29%M,	22%T,	17%S
Los Angeles	6972	.254	.260	.355	26%M,	22%T,	21%S
Philadelphia	4843	.271	.282	.390	26%M,	20%T,	20%S
Detroit	4212	.321	.291	.420	34%M,	21%T,	18%S
Boston	3773	.283	.297	.316	23%T,	23%S,	22%M
San Francisco	3122	.288	.309	.299	20%T,	20%S,	15%SL
Washington	2468	.452	.323	.435	30%F,	25%FM,	23%S
Pittsburgh	2386	.331	.325	.393	29%M,	21%T,	19%S
St. Louis	2356	.276	.325	.373	28%M,	21%T,	19%S

[a]Population estimates are from the Bureau of the Census.

[b]All federal employment and hotel and motel employment were assigned to basic. The data used are from *County Business Patterns* and from special tabulations available from the Bureau of Economic Analysis.

[c]The equation presented by Moore (1975), equation (2.20) in this paper, was used with the 1972 population estimate.

[d]Agriculture, mining, and federal employment were assigned to basic, as well as a share of state and local government employment equal to that state government's share of state and local government expenditure.

[e]The three sectors shown are those divisions with the most employment in each SMSA: The underlying data are an employment series available upon request from the Bureau of Economic Analysis, U.S. Department of Commerce (see Isserman, 1979). The abbreviations used here and in subsequent tables are: M = manufacturing, S = services, T = trade, F = federal civilian, FM = federal military, and SL = state and local government. Altogether there are twelve sectors, but only these six were ever in the largest three.

generates a monotonically increasing basic share related inversely to population, the location quotient shows no such regularity. In fact, Washington, New York, Pittsburgh, and Detroit (eighth, first, ninth, and fifth in population respectively) have the largest basic sectors. Those rankings conform quite nicely with the popular images of those cities as specializing in government, trade and services, steel, and automobile production. Indeed, while perhaps correcting for variations related to size, the minimum requirements approach is insensitive to the considerable variations in economic structure within size groups (as reflected by the division level profiles in the last column of table 2-2 and succeeding related tables). Note that Pittsburgh and St. Louis have the same minimum requirement estimate but vary by more than 20 percent in the location quotient estimate. Similarly, Chicago and St.

Louis have almost the same basic share from the structural perspective of the location quotient, but they have a 25 percent difference in basic share according to the population perspective of the minimum requirement.

The assignment estimate is larger than the location quotient estimate for eight of the ten cities. The particular assignment scheme used is lower than the location quotient only for New York and Washington, an expected result given the service specialization of those economies. The assignment scheme yields a higher estimate than the minimum requirement in all cases except that of San Francisco, another economy relatively specialized in trade and services which are assumed to be nonbasic. Before generalizing, however, it is worthwhile to examine the results for the other group of cities.

The cities shown in table 2–3 have relatively large concentrations of federal government employment, ranging from 15 to 42 percent of total employment in military or civilian employment alone. Here the location quotient estimate is uniformly higher than the minimum requirement — by more than 15 percentage points, or roughly one-third, in the extreme case of Fayetteville. If the minimum requirement approach is to be useful for cities of this kind, a modification to include all federal employment as basic would seem to be mandatory. The underestimation tendency of the location quotient is reinforced in these cities, since local consumption per employee is probably lower for federal military employees because of on-post consumption.

The assignment estimate is lower than the location quotient in three of the six federal center cases and lower than the minimum requirement twice; it has the greatest range. In all, this group of cities shows dramatically that the choice of bifurcation technique does matter a great deal in terms of the resultant impact multiplier.

Table 2–3.   Basic share of wage and salary employment, 1972, as estimated by alternative bifurcation techniques—federal centers

SMSA[a]	Pop. 1972 (1000's)	LQ	MR	A	Three largest sectors		
San Diego	1423	.431	.356	.451	20%FM,	18%S,	17%T
Pensacola	257	.475	.458	.434	17T%T,	15%FM,	16%S
Huntsville	231	.502	.464	.481	26%S,	20%F,	16%M
Fayetteville	210	.626	.470	.742	42%FM,	13%T,	11%M
Anchorage	142	.523	.493	.484	21%FM,	16%T,	15%S
Lawton	100	.599	.514	.628	39%FM,	15%T,	13%F

[a]For explanation of symbols, see table 2–2.

In the next group of cities, state capitals and/or university towns, the minimum requirement generates higher estimates than the location quotient in six of the seven cases, but in every case the difference in the estimates is less than 15 percent. The assignment estimate is sharply below the other two estimates in all but one case (Ann Arbor, which has a sizeable manufacturing sector), reflecting the omission of services and trade from the basic sector.

Table 2-4. Basic share of wage and salary employment, 1972, as estimated by alternative bifurcation techniques—state capitols and/or universities

SMSA[a]	Pop. 1972 (1000's)	LQ	MR	A	Three largest sectors		
Austin	327	.400	.444	.321	27%Sl,	20%T,	19%S
Madison	295	.391	.450	.341	33%SL,	20%T,	16%S
Ann Arbor	239	.468	.462	.512	33%SL,	31%M,	13%T
Champaign	162	.479	.485	.419	28%SL,	19%T,	15%FM
Gainesville	116	.496	.506	.341	43%SL,	18%T,	13%S
Tallahassee	114	.470	.507	.278	42%SL,	19%T,	18%S
Columbus, Mo.	82	.483	.526	.301	42%SL,	16%S,	15%T

[a]For explanation of symbols, see table 2-2.

In manufacturing cities (table 2-5), the location quotient estimate is lower than the minimum requirement estimate in all but the two largest cities. Perhaps in manufacturing the no-crosshauling assumption is most

Table 2-5. Basic share of wage and salary employment, 1972, as estimated by alternative bifurcation techniques—manufacturing cities

SMSA[a]	Pop. 1972 (1000's)	LQ	MR	A	Three largest sectors		
Rochester	888	.386	.384	.469	39%M,	18%T,	17%S
Flint	505	.466	.418	.514	43%M,	20%T,	13%SL
Canton	372	.399	.436	.462	40%M,	20%T,	16%S
Erie, Pa.	271	.359	.455	.500	43%M,	18%T,	18%S
Battle Creek	141	.487	.494	.492	37%M,	16%T,	16%S
Muncie	133	.400	.497	.581	35%M,	22%T,	15%S
Kenosha	120	.410	.504	.512	42%M,	18%T,	16%S
Danville, Il.	97	.426	.516	.474	36%M,	18%S,	17%T

[a]For explanation of symbols, see table 2-2.

problematic, suggesting that the technique might be modified to treat more or even all manufacturing as basic. The assignment approach generates the highest estimates in all but the smallest city in the group, which is a continuation of the pattern observed in table 2-2 for all six cities in which manufacturing is the largest sector.

Finally, in the eight selected sunbelt cities (table 2-6), all of which have services or trade as the largest sector, the minimum requirement is lower than the location quotient in half the cases. The most specialized city in the group by common notion is Las Vegas, which has the largest basic share by the location quotient approach. Minimum requirements are impervious to such specialization, but here, as in the three other cases where the minimum requirement is lower, the difference is less than 15 percent. In contrast, the assignment estimates are well below all the others, reflecting their insensitivity to trade and services.

Table 2-6.   Basic share of wage and salary employment, 1972, as estimated by alternative bifurcation techniques—selected sunbelt cities

SMSA[a]	Pop. 1972 (1000's)	LQ	MR	A	Three largest sectors		
Atlanta	1458	.389	.354	.265	27%T,	19%S,	16%M
Miami	1340	.351	.359	.225	26%S	25%T	13%M
San Antonio	909	.391	.382	.429	20%T	17%S	15%FM
Honolulu	654	.436	.402	.383	20%T	19%T	13%M
Orlando	480	.361	.421	.277	24%S	23%T	11%SL
Las Vegas	298	.491	.441	.176	43%S	18%T	10%SL
Sarasota	136	.407	.496	.167	27%S	27%T	12%SL
Reno	132	.415	.498	.149	36%S	21%T	13%SL

[a]For explanation of symbols, see table 2-2.

2.6 CONCLUSION

The results discussed in the previous section have a number of implications. First, a particular assignment scheme should not be applied universally without careful consideration of the nature of the regions under study. Although manufacturing and federal employment have been two important bases of economic development, the identity of the basic sector across American cities is far more varied: trade and service exporting cities must be recognized.

Estimates of basic activity that stem from bifurcation by assignment and do not assign any services or trade to the basic sector may be seriously flawed for such cities. Similarly, tests of the economic base model which incorporate estimates of basic employment derived by such bifurcation may be using very questionable data. What appear to be failures of the model may very well derive from failure to bifurcate adequately. Again, this criticism is particularly relevant to the mechanical application of the assignment approach using "universal" rules and is not a criticism of "custom-made" assignment based on knowledge of a region.

The underlying premise of the location quotient approach, that economic structure or specialization indicates basic activity, is probably a sound one; the variations in the basic share reflect that specialization.[8] Yet, although the resulting variations across regions seem reasonable, the technique has by definition a false central tendency related to gross versus net activity. However, since that tendency is systematic, it can be corrected.

Equation (2.8) of the location quotient approach becomes:

$$X_{ir} = \frac{E_{ir}}{E_{in}} - m \frac{E_r}{E_n} E_{in} \tag{2.23}$$

where m is the portion of the region's consumption which is from the region's production. Estimating m so that the equation measures gross exports remains an important research challenge; a successful method could improve bifurcation attempts immensely. Indeed, minimum requirements can be considered an unconvincing strategy for specifying m.

The estimates presented here show that there are considerable variations in economic structure across cities, beyond those controlled for by size, in the minimum requirement approach. Whereas its central tendency over all may be preferable to the location quotient, it is insensitive to relative specialization within population size groups. It needs to incorporate these other aspects of specialization, and in its present form probably should not be used for cities known to be highly specialized. On the other hand, given that the location quotient probably underestimates, the minimum requirement deviated in the right direction 79 out of 101 times. Whether it was more accurate remains unknown.

In sum, empirical results show considerable variation. The choice of technique does make a difference. No conclusive measure of comparative accuracy exists, and the theoretical rationales behind each approach are flawed. Thus, the practitioner and researcher must tread gingerly. Until better empirical evidence exists, probably the best strategy for the practitioner is to know the data for his area, and either to construct a hybrid approach or to compare the results of each approach, discarding those estimates which are lower than the location quotient. Similarly, the location quotient may be used as an upper bound for the multiplier if a facility closure is being studied. Also, a "sensitivity" approach noting the differences among estimates may well indicate industries which ought to be surveyed directly. A researcher working with cross-section data and without time for such "custom" bifurcation should be aware of the bias generated by the choice of bifurcation technique, and may be well advised to prune his data base to eliminate certain regions.

NOTES

1. The discussion is in terms of employment, the most readily available measure in the United States of industry-specific economic activity on the substate level; however, economic base analysis can also be carried out in terms of income, expenditure, output, or other measures of economic activity.
2. The population ratio P_r/P_n can be used instead of E_r/E_n, in which case per capita consumption is assumed to be equal in the region and nation.
3. This procedure will result in identical estimates of the basic share of total employment in all regions in the size class, since the same sum of minimum shares is assigned to nonbasic in each region. The industry-specific basic shares, however, will vary across regions.
4. As Hoyt (1961), Ullman, Dacey, and Brodsky (1969), and Brodsky and Sarfaty (1977) point out, the difference between the minimum requirement estimate of gross basic and the location quotient estimate of net basic may be considered to be an estimate of imports.
5. The areas were not selected randomly, but were used in Isserman (1977a) because of the availability of input-output tables for them.
6. Brodsky and Sarfaty similarly derived an equation for Nicaragua municipios. Their equation, $-39.77 + 14.30$ log Pop, predicts far smaller nonbasic sectors than the U.S. equation, as one would expect.
7. At the time of Leven's study the locus of basic activity within an economy was of primary interest.
8. The basic share can be shown to equal the coefficient of specialization, a measure of overall economic specialization (Isserman, 1977a).

3 THE MINIMUM REQUIREMENTS TECHNIQUE OF ESTIMATING EXPORTS: A FURTHER EVALUATION

Richard L. Pfister*

3.1 INTRODUCTION

The purpose of this paper is to provide further evaluation of the minimum requirements technique for estimating local export activity in economic base studies, and to present an application that seems to be free of most criticisms of the technique. The application is to estimate the sales of certain goods and services to tourists in metropolitan areas.[1] The location quotient does not yield reliable estimates of exports to tourists. The argument of this paper is that minimum requirements yields better estimates of exports to tourists, but yields less reliable estimates of exports of goods than does the proper use of the location quotient. The bulk of the paper deals with the application of minimum requirements to estimating export sales to tourists.

Ullman and Dacey (1960) argue that the minimum requirements technique is better than the location quotient and its variations for identifying export employment in cities. The minimum requirements technique consists of calculating the percentage distribution of employment by industrial category for each of several cities in a group.[2] The lowest percentage of employ-

*Professor of Business Economics, Indiana University.

ment in each industrial category for any city in the group is assumed to be the minimum percentage employment required for any city in the group to be "viable." "The minimum requirement closely approximates the service or internal needs of a city, and the excess employment approximates the export or base employment."[3]

Richard Pratt (1968) points out the shortcomings of the minimum requirements approach. He shows that it leads to a paradox, in that all cities are assumed to be exporting but none is assumed to be importing. In addition, the minimum requirements approach is subject to the same criticisms as the location quotient. Pratt concludes that the minimum requirements approach is less satisfactory than the location quotient for identifying export activity.[4]

3.2 SERVICES SUSCEPTIBLE TO THE TECHNIQUE

Despite the preceding criticism of minimum requirements, certain services come close to satisfying the necessary conditions for meaningful use of the technique. Such services must not be transportable and must generally be supplied at or near the residences (permanent or temporary) of the consumers. Examples are the installation and maintenance of telephones, plumbing fixtures, and household appliances; the servicing and repair of automobiles; and the maintenance and repair of houses. Other such services are those provided by hotels and motels, eating and drinking places, gasoline stations, and amusement places. These services are generally not transportable: users must consume them at the site of production, and this site is generally in the city of either the permanent or temporary residence of the consumer.[5] Most cities, and certainly all metropolitan areas, would supply them to their local residents, so no city of substantial size will show a zero minimum requirement for them.

The total sales of establishments serving visitors will, of course, include sales to local residents. Residents of a community patronize local eating and drinking places, gasoline service stations, and amusement places. And they require hotel and motel services for use by friends, relatives, and business representatives (salespersons, buyers, consultants, etc.) who need overnight accommodations. Such visitors will also consume services of other businesses serving visitors. These purchases by friends, relatives, and business representatives are here considered "indirect" requirements of local residents. Local production in excess of the direct and indirect requirements by local residents would then be exported by being sold to tourists. Most definitions of tourists include those persons visiting friends and relatives, so the measured excess (by the procedure suggested here) would understate total sales to tourists as usually defined. In other words, the minimum requirement as here defined would include sales to some tourists — primarily those visiting friends and relatives — in addition to the sales directly to local residents and to persons coming to the city for business purposes.

3.3 SIZE CLASSES AND MINIMUM REQUIREMENTS

Ullman and Dacey grouped cities into six population size groups for their calculations. They found that the minima became larger as cities increased in size. The authors stated that "This finding is consistent with theory, since the larger the city the larger the number of specialties that can be supported and the more self-contained the city can be."[6] The theory is that the market for certain specialties must be of a threshold size before production will occur. Diseconomics of small scale-plants prevent production from occurring in markets smaller than the threshold size. Small cities thus do not provide a large enough market to support production of some specialities. Their residents must either go without the speciality or import it from a larger city.

If the minimum requirements increase with city size because cities become more self-contained, these larger cities will then import relatively less. As their minimum requirements become larger, they will presumably export less — or at least this technique will identify fewer exports than it would if the minimum requirements had been lower. But the effect of city size on minimum requirements is not obvious. Is there any reason to expect larger cities to require a larger (or a smaller) percentage of their employment in providing services to their local residents? Larger cities may have more specialized and more expensive restaurants because of a threshold factor; namely, they have enough well-to-do customers or expense-account customers to support such establishments. Similarly, large cities may have specialized amusement parks while small cities do not. But even the smaller cities will have some establishments in each of the service categories examined in this study. And those cities above the threshold size for certain specialized services within each category are undoubtedly exporting some such services to cities below the threshold. But it is not clear that the larger cities should have higher minimum requirements for services.

There appears, however, to be another more important factor that would cause minimum requirements to vary with the size of a city or metropolitan area. The demand by local residents for the same type of services consumed by tourists is probably related positively to income. Because incomes are higher in the larger cities, we might therefore expect the larger cities to have a larger percentage of their employment in these services just to supply local requirements of local residents. It would be possible to make a rough adjustment to allow for this income effect where incomes differ significantly among cities. No such adjustment was made, however, in the calculations in this study. Rather, the calculations were made for four different groups based on population. Income differences within the four groups should be much smaller than among all SMSAs. Thus, the stratification by size should hold income relatively constant within each stratum.

To get a high average percentage for exports among a group of SMSAs, one or a few SMSAs must have very low minimum requirements or very small location quotients relative to the rest of the group. With the smaller SMSAs, it is more likely to find one (or a few) with a very low location quotient relative to the others. A skewed distribution of location quotients will thus lead to high average export percentages. The skewness is probably less for the groups of larger SMSAs, which could be at least partly the result of the threshold effect. Applying the minimum requirements technique for groups of small cities (under 50,000 population) would likely lead to the situation of one or a few cities having a zero minimum for highly disaggregated activities. Thus, it would lead to excessively large estimates of export activity for most of the small cities. Either the technique should be restricted to larger cities or the cities with very low minima should be discarded from the sample.

3.4 CALCULATING MINIMUM REQUIREMENTS

3.4.1 An Application

The usual method of calculating minimum requirements is to find the percentage of total employment accounted for by the selected activities in each city. Previous calculations of minimum requirements used employment data from the decennial *Census of Population,* which gives total employment and its breakdown by rather broad industrial categories. These categories are too aggregative to show data for the individual service activities catering to tourists. The best source of data for the selected services is in the *Census of Business,* but its dates do not coincide with those for the *Census of Population.* Consequently, comparable employment data for all employees and for industrial categories other than those given in the *Census of Business* are not readily available for the years of this census. Also, employment data in the *Census of Business* are for the week ending nearest November 15; employment for one week is apt to differ substantially from the average weekly employment for the year in the seasonal tourist-serving businesses. Use of data from the *Census of Business* therefore requires a different technique than that generally employed in calculating minimum requirements.

3.4.2 An Alternative Technique

This alternative technique relies upon location quotients. The city having the lowest location quotient is assumed to be supplying only its internal needs, that is, its minimum requirements. The denominator of the fraction yielding the location quotient for an SMSA is its percentage of total population among a group of SMSAs. The numerator is the percentage for the given SMSA of the group total for receipts (although it could be any other measure of the activity) in a given service category. Receipts or sales appear conceptually to be the best measure for these services. Annual payrolls are available, but receipts reflect returns to factors other than just labor. (They also include, of course, purchase of intermediate goods.) But these service establishments — hotels, eating and drinking places, amusements, gasoline service stations — probably vary slightly if at all in vertical integration. Thus, sales should reliably measure the relative activity among a group of such firms.[7]

The division of a city's share of receipts for a given service by its share of the group population yields its location quotient. This procedure assumes that the same receipts/resident ratio is necessary in all cities in the group to provide the minimum requirements. Differences in receipts per capita are accounted for by exports.[8]

A simple calculation provides the percentage of receipts that is attributed to tourists. The calculation consists of subtracting the smallest location quotient among the cities in the group from the location quotient for a given city, and dividing the result by that city's location quotient.

This technique for estimating minimum requirements and exports is not the same as that of using percentage distributions of employment for all the cities. It is similar, however, because it assumes that the city with the smallest location quotient is just supplying the needs of its local residents and that any city with a location quotient larger than the minimum is exporting the service. If prices of the services differ among cities, the calculation based on receipts will overstate the quantity of exports by cities that have higher prices.

If room rates are 50 percent higher in one city than in the other, that city with the higher rate will show greater exports, whereas both cities may actually be exporting the same amount. A similar problem arises in using employment as the measure of the activity. Then the implicit assumption is that employees in all cities have the same productivity. With respect to prices, there is probably a positive association between city size and price levels. If so, this association would be a good argument for calculating location quotients and minimum requirements by size-group of city. Otherwise, the calculations based on receipts would overstate exports of cities with higher prices — presumably the larger cities.

The two methods of calculating minimum requirements will yield the same export percentage for a given category if the receipts per employee are constant among cities — and if total employment is a constant proportion of population for all cities. Obviously these conditions will not exist, although the variations among cities may not be great. A check for 1963 showed that the two methods yielded close to the same export percentages for lodging establishments and for eating and drinking places in those SMSAs for which data were available to make both calculations. For amusements, however, receipts generally give a much higher export percentage than does employment. Apparently, employment for the week ending nearest November 15 greatly understated the yearly activity in this industry. For gasoline service stations, employment consistently gave a higher export figure than did receipts, and in many cases the difference was substantial. Service stations probably do not vary their employment much during the year — they can handle the additional sales during peak periods without much addition to their work force. They simply have excess capacity during off-peak periods. In all of these cases, however, receipts appear to be superior to employment for calculating exports by the minimum requirements method.

3.4.3 The Empirical Findings

The alternative technique for calculating minimum requirements was employed in calculations for all SMSAs and for four different size groups. The results presented in the first part of this section came from an earlier study, which covered the years 1954, 1958, and 1963. The calculations were updated for one size class (300,000 to 1,000,000 population) to include 1967 and 1972. These more recent results are presented in the latter part of this section.

3.4.3.1 All SMSA's. Table 3-1 shows the percentages of receipts in the four categories that were exported or sold to tourists. The number of SMSAs included in the calculations was 217 in 1963, 187 in 1958, and 172 in 1954. Table 3-1 gives the unweighted average export percentages for all SMSAs in each of the three years. The standard errors appear in parentheses below the averages. As expected, the average export percentages are highest for lodging (hotels-motels), ranging from 87.4 percent in 1958 to 91.3 percent in 1963. Amusement was the second highest, with the average export percentages ranging from 76.4 percent in 1964 to 88.4 percent in 1954. Eating and drinking places were next followed by gasoline service stations.

The 1954 figure for amusements seems high relative to 1958 and 1963, but the figure most out of line is that for eating and drinking places in 1954. The cause in both cases was that one SMSA turned up with an unusually low location quotient or minimum requirement. When this occurs, the export percentages of the other SMSAs come out high. Such unusually small location quotients raise doubts about the reliability of the data for the SMSAs involved. There is probably a good case for excluding such extremes

Table 3-1. Average export percentages and standard errors for selected services, all SMSAs 1963, 1958, and 1954[a]

Service category	1963	1958	1954
Hotels, motels	91.3	87.4	89.6
	(6.0)	(9.7)	(8.1)
Amusements	76.4	80.9	88.4[b]
	(10.4)	(8.5)	(6.5)
Gasoline service stations	44.1	42.1	39.4
	(10.5)	(10.4)	(11.8)
Eating and drinking places	62.5	63.5	86.4[b]
	(12.6)	(10.0)	(4.3)

[a]The averages are unweighted. Standard errors are in parentheses below the averages.

[b]One SMSA had an unusually small location quotient in 1954 for amusements and another for eating and drinking places. As a result, the export percentages were substantially higher for 1954 than for the other years for these two activities.

Source: Calculations based on data from U.S. Bureau of the Census, *Census of Business* for the indicated year.

in calculating the export percentages, although this was not done for table 3-1. Had they been excluded, the figures for 1954 would have been closer to those for 1958 and 1963, since for 1958 and 1954, the same SMSAs appeared among those with the highest and lowest export percentages (except for those areas too small to be classified as SMSAs in the earlier years), although rankings of the SMSAs did change over the three census years.

For amusements, Brownsville, Texas, was the city with the minimum requirement in 1963; next lowest in export percentages were Lake Charles, Louisiana (36.3), Abilene (48.0), Baton Rouge (49.5), and Lowell (52.6). The city with the highest export percentage was Reno (99.6) followed by Las Vegas (99.5) and Atlantic City (96.6). Others with high export percentages were New York (7th place with 93.2), Fort Lauderdale (9th with 92.8), Miami (10th with 92.6), and Chicago (22nd with 87.2).

The mean export percentage for gasoline service stations in 1963 was 44.1. Brownsville again had the minimum requirement; New York was the next lowest (8.8). Highest in the export percentages was Las Vegas (77.2).

For eating and drinking establishments, the mean export percentage was 62.5 in 1963. Gadsen, Alabama, had the minimum requirement; others with low percentage exports were Tyler, Texas (16.5), Brownsville (17.6), Laredo (19.0), Lake Charles (20.6), and Pine Bluff (27.2). Baltimore had the highest export percentage — 97.3; next was a surprise — Albany, Georgia (94.1); following, in order, were Atlantic City (88.5), Las Vegas (84.6), Reno (81.1), New York (81.0), and San Francisco (79.6).

Many of the SMSAs with low export percentages for amusements, gasoline service stations, and eating and drinking places probably had high proportions of low-income families. Thus their permanent residents would consume less of these services than other SMSAs with relatively fewer low-income households. If this assumption is correct, the minimum requirements of SMSAs should, of course, be adjusted for differences in income. The calculations as made, without such an adjustment, overstate the exports of SMSAs with higher incomes and understate the exports of those with the lower incomes.

3.4.3.2 Size groups.   The calculation of average export percentages for SMSAs grouped by size showed the combined effect on minimum requirements of several factors related to size — income, prices, productivity, threshold effects, etc. In most cases, the average export percentages for each size group were considerably smaller than for all SMSAs taken together (table 3-2). This result suggests that the SMSAs within groups had characteristics that differed significantly from those of other groups, and from those of all SMSAs combined. This suggestion was verified by an F-test showing the differences between groups to be statistically significant.

Table 3-2. Export percentages for selected services, all SMSA's and size groups, 1963

SMSA size group	Hotels, motels	Amusements	Gasoline service stations	Eating & drinking places
All SMSAs	91.3	76.4	44.1	62.5
Over 1,000,000	75.8	46.6	36.1	27.4
300,000 to 1,000,000	60.9	48.3	37.3	39.8
100,000 to 300,000	90.7	72.8	44.4	59.6
Under 100,000	78.9	39.0	26.8	54.6

Source: Calculations based on data from the U.S. Bureau of the Census, Census of Business.

A surprising result was that the 100,000–300,000 size group had the highest export percentages for all four of the service activities. The largest size group (1,000,000 and over) ranked third for hotels, amusements, and gasoline service stations, but ranked fourth for eating and drinking places. The smallest size group (SMSAs under 100,000) ranked second in export percentages for lodging and eating and drinking places, but fourth in amusements and gasoline service stations. If the minimum requirements rise with the size of the city, as Ullman and Dacey suggest, the largest size group would probably show the lowest export percentage. Conversely, the smallest size group would have the lowest minimum requirements, would probably have the greatest variability in location quotients, and thus would show the highest export percentages. The group 100,000 to 300,000 would be expected to have the second highest export percentages rather than the highest. In summary, table 3-2 does not support the hypothesis that minimum requirements rise (and exports fall) with city size. But there were significant differences among the groups in their export percentages. Perhaps the use of more groups with a narrower range of population would more clearly reveal the effect of size on minimum requirements and the export percentages.

3.4.3.3 Elimination of "special cases." The small export percentages in lodging for several of the New England SMSAs may be the result of their being close to other larger SMSAs, or of their being old industrial towns not attractive to visitors (Fall River, for instance). Patterson-Passaic grew largely as a satellite to New York City, and undoubtedly relies heavily on New York for services required by visitors. Because nine New England SMSAs and Patterson-Passaic are so far below the mean, it is tempting to discard them as special cases. To do so would be arbitrary, of course, but then so are many other decisions that are accepted without question, such as the delimiting of SMSAs. A better solution would probably be to include the New England SMSAs with the nearby larger SMSAs, or to explain the export percentages with a regression equation in which distance to the nearest larger SMSA is an explanatory variable. Neither of these solutions was attempted in this study.

Discarding these ten SMSAs dropped the mean export percentage for all SMSAs from 91.3 to 64.0 (table 3-3), but the top exporting city (Las Vegas) dropped only from 99.8 to 99.3. Table 3-3 also shows the effects on the mean export percentages by size group of eliminating the ten cities with the lowest minimum requirements. The declines were large for every group except one — the category 300,000 to 1,000,000. The adjusted figures were much closer together, ranging only from 49.0 to 60.3. The 100,000 to 300,000 group remained the one with the highest export percentage, and the over-1,000,000 group remained in third place. The other two groups, however, switched places, with the under-100,000 group moving from second to fourth.

Amusements, gasoline service stations, and eating and drinking places had only two instances (both in 1954) of exceptionally low-activity SMSAs. Consequently there was less temptation to discard certain of the SMSAs as unusual or unique cases that greatly influenced the export percentages. In fact, except for the two cases in 1954, the elimination of the low exporters for these services actually reduced the export percentages by 2 percent or less.

Table 3-3. The export percentages for hotels and motels unadjusted and adjusted[a] by size groups, 1963

Grouping of SMSAs	No SMSAs eliminated	Adjusted by eliminating extremely low exporters
All SMSAs	91.3	64.0
Over 1,000,000	75.8	51.9
300,000–1,000,000	60.9	56.0
100,000–300,000	90.7	60.3
Under 100,000	78.9	49.0

[a]The adjustment consisted of eliminating ten cities; all but one in New England had very low location quotients for hotels and motels.

3.4.4 An Updating

The preceding calculations were made several years ago as part of a larger study. Since that study was completed, two more *Censuses of Business* have been issued. The calculations were brought up to date by including 1967 and 1972 along with 1963 for one SMSA size-group — that of 300,000 to 1,000,000 population. The results of the new calculations are shown in table 3–4. The calculations for 1963 are new in table 3–4, and are slightly different than those in table 3–2. The differences, which are small, resulted from revisions of data since the earlier study and from changes in the definitions of a few SMSAs.

The mean export percentage would appear to be rising over time for these service activities. As income rises, expenditures on these travel-related activities could be expected to rise at a more rapid rate than income. Some of the changes in table 3–4 could be the result of data irregularities, particularly when one or a few SMSAs showed very low location quotients. In order to check on this possibility, the export percentages were recalculated after excluding the three SMSAs with the lowest location quotients for each activity. The adjusted figures are in table 3–5.

For lodging establishments, the adjusted figures are lower for all three years. The rising trend still shows up, but the rate of increase is much lower. This adjustment would seem to be desirable for lodging establishments, as the resulting figures are more stable and more in line with a priori expectations.

Table 3–4. Mean export percentages[a] for selected services, SMSAs between 300,000 and 1,000,000 for 1963, 1967, and 1972

Service category	1972	1967	1963
Hotels, motels	68.7	69.5	60.0
	(18.6)	(18.0)	(20.0)
Amusements	69.7	58.4	46.5
	(14.5)	(18.4)	(19.3)
Gasoline service stations	50.5	55.5	36.1
	(11.0)	(12.2)	(12.2)
Eating and drinking places	52.3	45.6	38.1
	(10.7)	(14.0)	(14.7)

[a]Unweighted averages: standard error is in parentheses.

Source: Based on data from U.S. Bureau of the Census, *Census of Business,* for the years indicated.

Table 3-5.   Adjusted mean export percentages[a]
for selected services, SMSAs between 300,000 and
1,000,000, 1963-1972

Service category	1972	1967	1963
Hotels, motels	61.2	58.9	56.0
	(20.2)	(18.9)	(19.1)
Amusements	57.2	59.8	47.2
	(17.2)	(16.8)	(19.2)
Gasoline service	44.2	57.1	36.4
stations	(8.8)	(9.7)	(12.0)
Eating and drinking	34.8	40.4	37.6
places	(12.0)	(13.7)	(14.8)

[a]Unweighted averages: standard errors in parentheses.
Source: Table 3-4.

The adjustment for amusements lowered the 1972 figure sharply but did not change the other two appreciably. The same observation applies to gasoline service stations.

The adjustment caused a substantial reduction in the export figures in 1972 and 1967 for eating and drinking places. The 1963 figure did not change much. Again this adjustment reduces volatility of the export percentages and brings them more in line with a prior expectations. It appears to make the figures for 1972 and 1967 more consistent with those for 1963.

The elimination of the three SMSAs with the lowest location quotients substantially reduced the volatility of the mean export percentages and made the trend seem more reasonable. Although this elimination is somewhat arbitrary, the low extremes cause unrealistic variations in the mean export percentages. The number of the extremes to eliminate can be determined only by examining the data and by using one's judgment. Elimination of the low extremes also greatly reduces the variation in mean export percentages among SMSAs of different sizes.

3.5 CONCLUSION

The question now arises as to how good are the results of this use of minimum requirements. The answer is uncertain because there are no true or correct figures with which to compare the results. There is cause for uneasiness because of the sensitivity of the export percentages to the exclusion of some SMSAs that might be considered special cases (or, what is perhaps the same, to the arbitrary definitions of SMSAs), and to the grouping by size. Elimination of the low extremes greatly reduces the variation in mean export percentages among the size classes.

It appears that minimum requirements is a useful technique for estimating exports of services to tourists. The estimates seem reasonable in light of the theory and in comparison with other techniques. The minimum requirements technique for estimating exports certainly makes more sense for these services than the simple location quotient (or average requirements). Each investigator will, however, have to use personal judgment in each case, in deciding what to include or exclude in the group of cities used to calculate the minimum requirement, and in deciding which low extremes to exclude.

NOTES

1. Disaggregated data are not always available for small economies because of the disclosure rules of data-collection agencies. Generally, one must supplement published data with unpublished data to achieve the desired disaggregation.
2. For areas large enough to be so classified, Ullman and Dacey use metropolitan areas. Throughout this paper, the term *city* refers to the metropolitan area for areas large enough to qualify for that designation.
3. Ullman and Dacey (1960), p. 176.
4. In his reply to Pratt, Ullman asserted that he and Dacey recognized in the original article that cities would be importing. While they did make such a statement, Pratt is correct in saying that imports are not allowed in the minimum requirements framework. Each city produces at least its own needs in every industrial category, and has excess employment in most categories, so it cannot be importing anything.
5. Obviously some such consumption occurs during day trips to cities well removed from the permanent or temporary residence of the consumer. I believe, however, that the qualified generalization in the text will still hold.
6. Ullman and Dacey (1960), p. 180.
7. Receipts might not be the best measure of the activity if the objective is to measure the local impact or local income generated rather than gross exports. A significant part of receipts might flow out of the community if the owners live outside because receipts include the return to capital. When outside ownership predominates, employment or payroll might be a better measure for determining local impact.
8. Communities might differ with respect to amusement and recreation facilities available to users at no charge; or if there is a charge, they might differ in the mix

between publicly and privately provided facilities. The census includes only privately operated enterprises, which, of course, charge for their facilities and services. Receipts and employment for publicly operated facilities (such as municipal parks or zoos) would be included in the local government sector. No information is available concerning the variation among cities with respect to these matters. The technique used here will understate exports for cities that have a greater than average proportion of publicly provided facilities and services.

4 ERROR GENERATION IN REGIONAL INPUT-OUTPUT ANALYSIS AND ITS IMPLICATIONS FOR NONSURVEY MODELS

Benjamin H. Stevens and Glynnis A. Trainer*

4.1 INTRODUCTION

There has recently been a dramatic increase in research on, and application of, regional input-output techniques. The need of many state governments and metropolitan planning agencies for workable economic models of their regions for use in measuring the economic and fiscal impacts of public and private investment decisions has been substantially increased by the growing issues of industrial shift, fiscal decline, environmental control, and energy planning.

The usefulness of regional input-output analysis for many of these purposes would appear to be well-established. However, there remain differences of opinion about the range of problems for which input-output is more appropriate than simpler, and cheaper, techniques such as economic base-multiplier analysis. And there are substantial questions about the use of input-output for long-term forecasting, for which econometric models may be significantly better suited.

*President and Research Associate, Regional Science Research Institute, Amherst, Massachusetts.

These issues cannot be resolved in the abstract. At a minimum, the cost-effectiveness of alternative techniques must be considered in the context of the problem to be analyzed and the types of measures desired. And the appropriateness of the technique chosen for a particular study is clearly influenced by whether the model is to be used once or repeatedly, since continuing use can make the "per unit" cost of a more complex model competitive with that of a simpler and perhaps less satisfactory approach.

In one sense, current practice, as described in the literature, does not reflect the actual possibilities of generating and using regional input-output models. Analysts appear to behave as if a satisfactory input-output model of a region will cost several orders of magnitude more than a base-multiplier model; and as if this cost is generally not warranted, despite the extensive impact detail which can be derived from input-output; and its value for use in other studies once it is constructed.

In apparent attempts to reduce costs, many analysts have expended substantial efforts on developing sophisticated methods of adapting and updating existing models, and have generally concentrated on trying to show that modest investments in nonsurvey models can provide usable results. When these results are compared with reality, however, they have often been found to be unsatisfactory.[1]

At the same time, cost considerations have led most survey-based models to be so highly aggregated as to raise questions about their usefulness in performing the functions for which input-output analysis was designed.[2]

It has long been the contention of the present authors and their associates that the adaptation of existing models need not be complicated or expensive; that the process of aggregation, especially in nonsurvey models, saves little in cost relative to the losses in information; and that many of the basic issues in the construction and use of regional input-output models have been ignored in favor of the methodological development of ever-more-complex approaches to the achievement of spurious accuracy. Repeated adaptation and use of the survey-based 490-sector, Philadelphia Region Input-Output Model for other regional economies has demonstrated that simple, straightforward, and inexpensive methods can provide satisfactory results at a high level of detail.[3]

The authors' recent work shows that the accuracy of such adapted models is more than acceptable for the purposes to which such models are appropriately put. And their comparison of the amounts of error generated in various components of such models suggests strategies for cost-effective survey data collection which might be employed in cases where some survey research is budgetarily feasible.

The purpose of this paper, therefore, is to discuss the implications of previous work on nonsurvey and small-survey regional input-output models for the future construction and use of such models. Special emphasis is given to the range of applicability of such models and to the multipurpose nature of both the adaptation procedure and the survey data which might be collected.

4.2 A BRIEF REVIEW OF ERROR GENERATION IN REGIONAL INPUT-OUTPUT

The authors' work, of particular relevance to this paper, consists of a series of simulation experiments.[4] Hypothetical regional input-output matrices of orders of 10, 25, 50, and 100 were generated. For each order of matrix, a hypothetical final demand column was also generated, and applied, in a round-by-round calculation, to the corresponding matrix, in order to calculate the total (direct, indirect, and induced) outputs by sector, as well as the overall output and wage multipliers.

After the initial calculation, the individual matrices were altered by the application of error to their coefficients. For each matrix, the technological coefficients of each of several altered matrices were drawn from a normal distribution whose mean was the original coefficient and whose standard deviation was variously a nominal 10 percent, 20 percent, 30 percent, or 40 percent of the original coefficient. After each of the coefficients in an input column was randomly drawn from the same error distribution, the column was renormalized so that the coefficients would add to a constant sum less than or equal to 1.0, as is necessary for the matrix to fulfill the requirements of input-output.

Each of the altered matrices was then used with the final demand vector associated with the original matrix in a new calculation of outputs and multipliers. Since one of the hypothetical "sectors" in each matrix is "households," employment and employment multipliers were also calculated. The results from using the error matrices were then compared with the "exact" solution, previously calculated.

Comparisons were made mainly through the use of the inequality coefficient U, calculated on the differences between the exact sector outputs and the outputs obtained for each of the altered matrices.[5] From a sample of 192 "error" matrices of various orders and error levels, a mean error of 26 percent in the matrix coefficients led to a mean U across the sample of .067 for outputs. The mean U's for the multipliers, using each error matrix as a single prediction, were .075 and .087 for the output and wage multipliers, respectively.

Unfortunately, the employment multipliers were not retained as part of the calculation so they could not be compared afterward. However, one would expect their errors to be similar to those of the output and wage multipliers.

The components of the various U's indicate that, in most cases, more than half of the error is caused by incomplete covariation, and less than one quarter is caused by errors of central tendency.[6] These results are to be expected, given the way in which the errors were generated.

There is a significant negative correlation of $-.314$ between the output U levels and the order of the matrix. This strongly suggests that disaggregation pays significant dividends in the accuracy of the results obtained from using an input-output model. This is no real surprise since it is well known that, in national models, aggregation creates mixtures of sectors which are not technologically commensurate, and which do not react uniformly to exogenous changes. But the loss of information and accuracy due to aggregation is even greater for regional models, as will be further discussed below.[7]

For the moment, it is worth noting that the errors due to both central tendency and unequal variation are also negatively and significantly correlated with matrix order, but the errors of incomplete covariation are not. Therefore, this latter type of error cannot, in general, be reduced by using a more disaggregated model.

4.3 ERROR REDUCTION AND MODEL STRUCTURE

The previous results were based on a set of experiments in which all elements in the model, except for the exogenous final demand column, were allowed to vary over the error distribution chosen for that experiment. Yet the probable sizes of errors could well vary among the model elements, and the ability to reduce errors through limited survey data collection also varies among the components of the model. Thus, if errors in certain model components have relatively larger effects on the accuracy of the results from using the model, this would provide guidance to the optimal use of limited survey funds.

To discuss these matters, it is necessary to describe the model structure which the authors and their associates used in their applied work, and which is simulated in the experiments previously described. The model is of the type designed mainly to measure the impacts of exogenous changes. Therefore, the discussion may not, in all respects be applicable to more general forecasting or dynamic models; nor does it deal with full-scale interregional models, in which the export demand by other regions for the products of the region in question are included as an integral part of the model.

The model has the following elements:

$A = [a_{ij}]$ a matrix of technological coefficients in units of cent's worth of input i per dollar's worth of input j, including:

$[a_{in}]$ a column of household purchase coefficients and:

$[a_{nj}]$ a row of labor input coefficients, where:

$0 \leq a_{ij} \leq 1$ for all i and j, and

$\sum_i a_{ij} \leq 1$ for all j;

$R = [r_i]$ a vector of regional purchase coefficients where:

$r_i =$ the proportion of input i, which is utilized by all industries and households in the region, and which is purchased from industry i in the region rather than imported from other regions, and

$0 \leq r_i \leq 1$ for all i.

Then, given a unit "final demand" vector:

$y = [y_i]$ where:

$0 \leq y_i \leq 1$ and

$\sum_i y_i \leq 1$ and where:

$y_i =$ the input requirement in cent's worth of input i per dollar's worth of a new, export, or other exogenous activity, and given:

$q =$ the scalar level of this activity (e.g., the number of dollar's worth of new output),

it is easy to calculate:

$X = [x_j]$ where:

$x_j =$ *the additional output of industry j* in the region, generated directly, indirectly, or induced, by the new activity.

This calculation can be accomplished using either the standard inverse of I-A, or the Leontief power series. For convenience in making further adjustments in the model without recalculating the inverse, the Leontief power series is often more practical. It also uses less computer time, and is less subject to round-off errors than is standard inversion, especially for large matrices.

For the purposes of this paper, the calculation is as follows:

$$X = [I + \tilde{R}A + (\tilde{R}A)^2 + \ldots + (\tilde{R}A)^k]\tilde{R}qY \qquad (4.1)$$

where:

I = identity matrix, and
$\tilde{R}$ = a diagonal matrix with the elements of R along the main diagonal and zeros elsewhere,

with:

$k \geq 8$, which is generally sufficient to reduce captured indirect and induced effects to less than .01 percent of x_{ji} for all j.

Then the output multiplier is:

$$M_o = \sum_j x_i/q$$

and the wage multiplier is:

$$M_w = x_n/qy_n. \qquad (4.3)$$

From the foregoing, and given additional information, other measures can be derived, such as the employment multiplier, occupational-skill demands, effluent loads, etc., generated directly or indirectly or induced by the exogenous final demand.

Note that the regional purchase coefficients, r_i, are specified only by the source industry, i. It may be possible in some cases to differentiate among the industries purchasing i as an input, according to the extent to which they obtain this input from inside or outside the region. As a practical matter, however, such differentiation is usually possible only with extensive and costly survey work. It is therefore assumed throughout the discussion that an input of a good i used in a region is drawn from a pool made up of the proportions r_i and $(1 - r_i)$, produced locally and imported, respectively.

The major components of the model in which error may be generated are: the technological coefficients $a_{ij}(i,j \neq n)$; the household purchase coefficients, a_{in}; the labor input coefficients, a_{nj}; and the regional purchase coefficients, r_i. The major variations among regions are in the r_i and the a_{in}, with the a_{nj}, and, especially, the a_{ij}, assumed to vary the least. This latter assumption, even if it is not totally justified, is often the only practical assumption to be made in adapting a model from another region or in using the U.S. national coefficients. Rarely are funds available to determine, through survey methods, interregional differences in entire production functions, although it is usually possible to use *Census* data to adjust some of the a_{nj}.

Fortunately, it happens that errors in the a_{ij} are relatively the least costly in terms of losses in the accuracy of the results. In the experiments run, an average of only 25 percent of the output error and 34 percent of the multiplier error was caused by errors in the coefficient matrix, exclusive of the household purchase column. Since the mean U for the outputs was .067, and for the multipliers, .081, this means that for an average of 26 percent error in the technological coefficients alone, a U of only about .016 and .027 was generated in the outputs and multipliers, respectively.

On the other hand, U's of about .050 and .040 were generated in the outputs and multipliers, respectively, by 26 percent mean errors in the household purchase coefficients alone. This suggests that reduction of error in the household column should be much more effective in reducing overall error than an equivalent reduction of error in the entire technological matrix.

The reason for these results is basically very simple. In open regional economies, the leakage of purchases out of the region is logically and demonstrably large, with correspondingly small r_i, for many material inputs. Therefore, a significant portion of the total indirect and induced effects of an exogenous change arise through the purchase of labor from households, for which the regional purchase coefficient, r_n, is generally close to 1. Other major sources of secondary effects are local trade and service sectors which tend both to be labor-intensive and to have much of their demand generated by wage payments to local households.

The foregoing suggests that errors in the estimation of the extent of purchase leakage should have relatively large effects on the accuracy of the results obtained from using regional input-output models. This is indeed true.

Experiments run with errors allowed only in the r_i indicated that a given mean error in the elements of R generates about three times as much error in the outputs, and about one and one-half times as much error in the multipliers, as the same mean error in the elements of A. If the A-matrix errors are limited to just the household purchase column, then errors in the input-output results can be ascribed almost entirely to errors in the regional purchase coefficients. This indicates that given errors in the estimation of regional leakage have a greater effect on the accuracy of estimation of the multiplier effect generated via households than do equivalent errors in the household purchase coefficients themselves.

It is worth considering the basic structure of the model in order to understand the logic underlying these results. Note first that the household purchase coefficients, like all the a_{ij}, are subject to the discipline that each column must sum to some constant less than or equal to 1. Thus an error which leads to a coefficient being too large must be compensated for by a proportional reduction in the size of one or more of the other coefficients in that column. Errors in the a_{ij}, therefore, are at least partially compensated for; too large a secondary effect via one sector is accompanied by reduced effects in other sectors.

On the other hand, the r_i are subject only to the requirement that they lie between 0 and 1. A regional purchase coefficient that is too large can increase secondary effects in the region without any automatic offsetting compensation. In fact, all of the r_i could simultaneously be too small or too large.

Thus it should not be surprising that, other things being equal, R-vector errors have the greatest relative effect on the accuracy of the results from using a regional input-output impact model. This conclusion is an additional argument for the greatest possible sectoral disaggregation.

At the four-digit SIC level, it is usually possible to identify, in a typical region, a substantial number of sectors for which the regional purchase coefficients are essentially equal to zero. This is so because it can be determined that there is no production of the outputs associated with those sectors in the region in question. At the same time, the detailing of trade and service sectors allows the analyst to differentiate between local service, retail, and government sectors, for which the r_i will generally be close to 1; and sectors such as wholesaling, finance, insurance, higher education, business services, etc., whose output may be purchased, to a relatively greater extent, from other regions.

4.4 IMPLICATIONS FOR NONSURVEY MODELS

The implications of the foregoing discussion for constructing "adapted" regional models should be clear.

1. The most detailed set of technological coefficients available should be used. These might be from the 485-sector U.S. Department of Commerce model. But there may be reasons for using the coefficient matrix from another region. For example, the authors and their associates generally use the Philadelphia Region matrix when constructing an adapted model for another metropolitan area. The argument for this approach is that metropolitan economies are in many ways dissimilar to the nation or states which contain them. One expects, for example, that a four-digit SIC sector in a metropolitan agglomeration will have more and larger inputs for secondary processing services, and perhaps smaller labor and other inputs, than the

national average for this sector, because specialized processes and services are farmed out. Large states, on the other hand, may have four-digit sectors which are relatively more self-contained, especially if they are outside the industrial Northeast.

2. The household purchase coefficients should be adjusted from those appearing in the table, and adapted to those appropriate for the region under study. For most large SMSAs, *Consumer Expenditure Study* data can be used directly. However, it may be necessary to modify these data or average over several SMSAs when estimating the a_{in} for a state or larger region.[8]

The adjustment procedure is generally very simple. Expenditure data, as reported, are aggregated into a small number of categories. These aggregates can be used as control totals for the detailed expenditure categories in the input-output table. Lacking other data, the detailed coefficients for the sectors comprising an aggregate are all adjusted in the same proportion, so that they sum to the control total.

3. The labor input coefficients are adjusted for all sectors for which wage and output data are both available from the *Census of Manufactures* or other sources. Again, lacking other data, all nonlabor coefficients in each column are adjusted proportionately so that the labor and nonlabor inputs sum to the same total as in the original table.

4. The regional purchase coefficients are estimated. Here, the importance of accuracy, and the usual lack of direct information on regional purchase patterns, warrant more extensive discussion.

4.4.1 Estimation of Regional Purchase Coefficients

Unfortunately, there is no magic way of making accurate estimates of the regional purchase coefficients, or even of checking on their accuracy, without extensive survey work. However, techniques have been developed and used that have some underlying theoretical appeal and appear to generate reasonable results. But these techniques must be considered tentative, subject to both test and revision when and as survey data become available for a reasonable sample of regions.

At the outset, it should be understood that the authors' empirical approach to this problem is conservative. When in doubt, they give the r_i a downward bias, since it is generally preferable to err on the side of underestimating the secondary regional impacts of exogenous changes. This bias may, of course, be an overreaction to the tendency, in many studies, to conclude that intraregional employment multipliers are as high as 2.5, 3.0, or even higher.[9] Multipliers this high are rarely realistic, either logically or empirically, for most open regions, because of the typically high level of purchase leakage.[10]

The r_i for most goods and some services can be estimated by systematic, if questionable, techniques. The traditional approach is to start with the location quotient.[11] A basic assumption is that a location quotient greater than 1 implies that a region should be self-sufficient in the good or service in question, and, thus, the sector should have an r equal, or close, to 1. The corollary assumption is that, for location quotients less than 1, r should reflect the actual value of the location quotient.

The rationale for these assumptions is simple. The location quotient expresses the region's percentage of total production taking place in the sector, relative to the national percentage of total production in that sector. Thus it can be assumed, for example, that a location quotient of .3 means that the region produces only 30 percent of the amount needed to fulfill its intermediate and final demands for the output of that sector. This implies further that these demands, per capita or per employee, in the region are the same as the national average.

Although the authors and their associates have, in the past, used location quotients as the basis for their regional purchase coefficients, there are certain conceptual problems involved in this approach.

The problems with location quotients have long been recognized.[12] To summarize briefly, the assumption that a location quotient of 1 implies regional self-sufficiency for the good or service in question may not be tenable. First, the consumption pattern of a region may differ from the national average because of climate, tastes, and, most especially, income. Second, the industrial demand for goods as inputs to production will depend upon the industrial structure of the region. For example, if the location quotient for steel in Detroit were as low as 1, the Detroit Metropolitan Region would doubtless not be self-sufficient in steel simply because of the very large regional demands for this product on the part of the automobile industry.

Third, *Census of Transportation* data indicate a high degree of interregional cross-hauling. Furthermore, the surveys done for the Philadelphia Region Input-Output Study showed that goods of which Philadelphia was a large producer and exporter were also imported into the region in substantial quantities. Thus, "excess" production of a good in a region, as implied by a large location quotient, is no guarantee that imports of that good will not be required.

Because of these deficiencies in regional purchase coefficients, a better technique has recently been suggested.[13] In this approach, the regional demands are not assumed to be the national averages but, rather, are calculated from the input-output structure of the region in question. For this purpose define:

$$\hat{r}_j \leq \frac{x_j}{d_j}$$ (4.4)

where:

$\hat{r}_j$ = the tentative or "base" regional purchase coefficient for sector j.[14]
d_j = the total intermediate and final demand in the region for the output of sector j.
x_j = the regional output of sector j.

The logic of this approach is transparent. If regional production exceeds regional demand, $\hat{r}_j$ will be tentatively estimated as close to 1. For a sector in which there is excess regional demand, $\hat{r}_j$ will reflect the need to import good j in order to fulfill regional needs. On the whole, this approach to the estimation of regional purchase coefficients seems straightforward and intuitively appealing.

Unfortunately, the d_j must be estimated, and this is not an entirely straightforward process. But at least it requires data which, for the most part, have to be assembled anyway in constructing an adapted model.

One major element in this calculation is the A-matrix, as adapted for the region including the household sector. Then define:

$D = [d_j]$
$Z = [z_j]$ which are the estimated "before-impact," steady-state, current, or otherwise most recent output levels, in dollar terms, in the region;
$A = [a_{ij}]$,the industry matrix.

Then:

$$D = AZ$$

Note that this requires only a single matrix multiplication rather than a full-scale input-output calculation; thus, the calculation of the d_j is neither difficult nor expensive. The problem in this approach is in obtaining the z_j, since output levels, in dollar values, are generally not directly available for many sectors in most regions. The major exceptions are usually those *Census of Manufactures* sectors for which data are available for value of shipments.

For other manufacturing sectors, and for nonmanufacturing, a variety of estimation techniques may have to be employed. The authors and their associates have had fair success with making estimations for those manufacturing sectors which do not appear in the *Census,* or which have disclosure problems, by using *County Business Patterns (CBP)* data. The approach used is to estimate employment by detailed sector, through an hierarchical decomposition of the data on the number of establishments in each size class of a sector and its subsectors, as reported in *CBP.*[15] Then, using the assumption that output/employee is the same in the estimated subsectors as in the aggregate sectors to which they belong, dollar output estimates can be generated for all manufacturing sectors.

For nonmanufacturing sectors, estimation is generally more difficult. For those sectors which appear in *CBP* and the *Census of Retail Trade, Wholesale Trade,* or *Selected Services,* total payroll and other measures are available. One approach to estimating output in such sectors is to use the relationship:

$$z_j = P_j / a_{nj} \tag{4.5}$$

where

P_j = total payroll in sector j; and

z_j and a_{nj} are as previously defined.

Subsectors which do not appear due to disclosure can have their payrolls estimated by *CBP* data, as previously described.

For sectors which appear only in *CBP,* data on payroll from this source must be used. These data are generally less satisfactory, in part due to underrepresentation of smaller establishments which may predominate in many trade and service sectors. Sometimes corrections for this underrepresentation are possible using *CBP,* or local, estimates of coverage.

It is sometimes possible to use *Census* sales data for retail and wholesale establishments in the estimation of outputs. This, of course, requires having good data on wholesale and retail margins, in order to convert sales into outputs. Margin is defined as the proportion of a dollar's worth of "sales" of a trade activity which pays for the operation and profits of the establishment rather than for the goods being traded. In most current input-output models, including the 485-sector U.S. model and the Philadelphia Region Model, the input coefficients of trade sectors are defined in cent's worth of input per dollar's worth of margin. The purchase of the actual goods in trade is then assigned directly to the sectors which produce the goods.

Given sales data as available from *Census, Sales Management,* and other sources, the "output" of a trade sector can then be estimated by multiplying its total sales by its margin coefficient. For the detailed sectors in SIC industries 50–59, this may provide the best estimate of output for use in the calculation of regional demand. Unfortunately, margin data are usually not available on a region-specific basis. Therefore, national average margins often must be used, thereby presumably generating some error in the output estimates.

Once all existing output levels z_j are estimated, and the calculation of the d_j completed, the $\hat{r}_j$ can be calculated. However, the $\hat{r}_j$, whether calculated from location quotients, the preceding technique, or some other method, are still estimates, and thus subject to further correction.

The most obvious correction is to take into account the extent to which shipments from a region stay within a region. A large supply/demand ratio for a good is irrelevant if much of the region's output of the good is being exported to other regions. Thus define:

s_j = proportion of the total value of j produced in the region which remains within the region;

then:

$$r_j = s_j \hat{r}_j. \qquad (4.6)$$

For states and production areas, data are available from the *Census of Transportation* for the proportions of many commodities and manufactured goods that are shipped to destinations within the state or production area in question. For other regional definitions, estimation procedures must be used, based on the data for the state or production area in which the region is included. Missing data and disclosure problems also require the use of estimates.

The authors have had reasonable success in making such estimates by employing the *Census of Transportation* data on the proportion of each good or commodity shipped, given distances from the state or production area of origin. Regression equations to explain these proportions have been fitted, using such independent variables as the weight/value ratio of the good in question, population density and income potential of the region, and related simple measures. The regression equations allow one to make estimates for various sizes and types of regions and for goods and commodities not listed in the *Census of Transportation* data.

For those trade and service activities for which shipment data would be unavailable, irrelevant, or both, other estimation procedures can be developed. However, experience with the supply/demand ratio technique described above suggests that it is most applicable to manufacturing sectors in any event. The errors inherent in transforming employment or sales data into output measures often appear to cause the supply/demand ratios for nonmanufacturing sectors to differ much further from 1 than seems reasonable. These estimated outputs are, of course, necessary to perform the calculation of the demands for all sectors, including manufacturing. But output errors in nonmanufacturing are unlikely to create large errors in the demands for manufactured goods, since the consumption of such goods as inputs is a very modest portion of the total value of output in most nonmanufacturing sectors.

As long as the household consumption column is properly estimated and good manufacturing output data are available, one can be relatively confident in the supply/demand ratios for manufacturing sectors. It then appears that it is often easier, and even more reasonable, to fall back on location quotients for trade and services. An important proviso is that such location quotients should, for retailing and services at least, be calculated in terms of sales or wages and income, rather than based simply on relative employment.

Another problem which has arisen in the application of this supply/demand technique is the fact that certain important "consumption" activities are not generally included in the static input-output framework. In particular, government purchases of goods and services from the region for use in the region, and the demands for goods and services for capital formation, are not included. In some regions these two types of demand, "external" to the input-output system, will add substantially to the denominator of the supply/demand ratio. The availability of input columns for a variety of state and federal government purchases and for capital formation in major two-digit SIC sectors makes it possible to correct for this deficiency in the supply/demand calculation and provide more accurate regional purchase coefficients.

4.5 IMPLICATIONS FOR SURVEY DATA COLLECTION

The foregoing discussion gives an indication of how limited survey funds should be allocated in constructing and using an adapted regional input-output model. First priority should be given to the collection of regional purchase data. The experience of the authors and their associates is that such data can be collected quickly and cheaply, often through a mail survey. However, interviews with major regional establishments, each of which can generally be completed with as little as one-half person-day of survey effort, are often worthwhile. Experience indicates that the geographic source of inputs is usually much less sensitive information than the input structure of the establishment itself; thus, most firms are willing to provide the required regional purchase data if they are able to. Unfortunately, many firms, especially the smaller ones, buy their material inputs from wholesalers in the region. The wholesalers themselves must often be surveyed in order to trace commodities back to their geographic source.

Second priority should be given, where appropriate, to directly capturing the "first-round" effects of an exogenous change. This approach can be understood most easily by reference to an example in an impact study of the General Dynamics shipyard in Quincy, Massachusetts. It was possible to obtain from the firm a list of its input suppliers.[16] This list provided information on the commodity description, the dollar amount, and, most important, the location of the supplier for each input purchase.

With these data it was possible to obtain an exact measure of the direct changes in the outputs of industries within the region which would be required to support a given change in the output of the shipyard. This "first-round" set of additional regional outputs could then be used as the "final demand" column in the input-output calculation of the remaining indirect and induced effects. For this latter purpose, errors in the estimated regional purchase coefficients would be less significant.

The increase in the accuracy of the results obtained by this "first-round" method is quite substantial. The error experiments, previously described, indicated that about 65 percent of the total output and multiplier effects of an exogenous change occur in the first round. If this seems high, recall that the leakage of some purchases from the region can be as high as 100 percent. This fact, in combination with the rapidly declining level of indirect and induced purchases attributable to each round of even a national model, leads to significant effects in the first round, relative to later rounds.

The implication of these results is that overall potential error can be reduced by more than one-half simply by having an accurate measure of first-round effects. In the shipyard study mentioned, the process actually was carried into the second round. The suppliers of the shipyard (other than households) were interviewed to determine the geographical source of *their* inputs. This permitted the calculation of an accurate set of total (aside from households) first- and second-round output changes to be used as the "final-demand" column for the rest of the input-output calculation. The total reduction in potential error has been estimated to be over 75 percent.

The foregoing approach is not applicable in cases where the exogenous change is the creation of a new activity whose detailed input structure (much less whose geographic purchase pattern) is not known at the time of the analysis. And even in the case of a change in an existing activity, it may not be known in advance how the change itself may affect regional purchase patterns. Nevertheless, the "first-round" approach may often be an inexpensive way of reducing error when using adapted input-output models.

As should be clear from the previous discussion, lower priorities should be given to collecting survey data on labor input coefficients, with other technological issues receiving the lowest priority of all. For the a_{ij} in general, and the a_{nj} in particular, preference as targets for survey efforts would obviously be given to larger firms in larger regional industries.

It is possible that system errors due to A-matrix errors may be so small that it would be difficult to ever again justify constructing a regional table based entirely on survey data. Certainly one could not expect a repetition of an effort on the scale of the Philadelphia study. And the survey-based state tables may lose through aggregation almost as much as they gain from access to original data.

However, it is likely that there are a small number of typical metropolitan technologies, state technologies, and other regional technologies varying broadly with size, industrial concentration and diversity, location, and other regional characteristics. The identification of a few such typical technologies, and limited survey research to establish their major technological differences, would help to assure that an appropriate A-matrix is available for adaptation to any particular region.[17]

Obviously, if information exists on technological differences between the table to be adapted and the region of application, this information should be used. At least the labor input coefficients can be determined from the *Census of Manufactures* data for total payroll and value of shipments.

4.6 CONCLUSION

This paper, and the research on which it is based, argues for highly detailed, but inexpensively adapted, regional input-output models employing an absolute minimum of survey data. This argument can be made more strongly for models to be used mainly for the evaluation of exogenously generated impacts, than for structural and forecasting models.[18] But in any case, diminishing returns set in rapidly in survey data collection for the construction of an input-output model for a particular region.

However, existing techniques for estimating regional purchase coefficients cannot be fully tested, nor can more accurate methods be developed, without some additional survey or *Census* data. Given the importance of the extent of regional leakage to the accuracy of input-output calculations, this would suggest the desirability of a much more comprehensive and detailed *Census of Transportation,* a sample survey of input sources for leading industries in a number of regions, or both.[19]

NOTES

1. See, for example, Czamanski and Malizia (1969), Malizia and Bond (1974), MacMenamin and Haring (1974), Morrison and Smith (1974), and Schaffer and Chu (1969).
2. See, for example, Bourque (1967, 1971b), Doekson and Little (1968), Fei (1956), Hewings (1972), and Morimoto (1970).
3. See, for example, Coughlin et al. (1977), Langford and Coughlin (1971), Steiker et al. (1976), and Stevens et al. (1975).
4. Stevens and Trainer (1976).
5. Following Theil (1966), the definition of U is:

    $$U = \left[\sum_i (P_i - A_i)^2 / \sum_i A_i^2 \right]^{1/2}$$

    where:

    A_i = the actual or "exact" output of sector i;
    P_i = the predicted or estimated output of i given errors in the matrix.

6. See Theil (1966).
7. For other discussions of aggregation errors in input-output, see Fei (1956), Hewings (1972), Morimoto (1970), Polenske (1974), and Williamson (1970).
8. See Bureau of Labor Statistics (n.d.).
9. See, for example, Grubb (1973).
10. Those readers concerned about the additional downward bias on outputs and multipliers caused by ignoring interregional feedback effects, as in the models discussed here, should refer to Miller (1969).
11. Usually defined [see Isard (1960)] as:

    $$LQ_i = (E_i / \sum_i E_i) / (E_i^n / \sum_i E_i^n)$$

    where:

    E_i and E_i^n are employments in sector i in the region and the nation respectively.

12. Compare Isard (1960).
13. See Treyz (1977).
14. Further adjustment of these "tentative" coefficients is described below.
15. For a detailed description of this technique, see Stevens et al. (1975).
16. Stevens et al. (1975).
17. For interstate differentials, see Polenske (1974).
18. Such as those for the state of Washington [c.f. Bourque et al. (1967, 1971b)].
19. For a cogent discussion of many of the major issues raised here, see Miernyk (1976). Miernyk clearly doubts the value of any adapted models. But he apparently agrees that accuracy in the estimation of direct and "first-round" effects is of crucial importance and is achievable through simple survey and interview methods. And he is a leading voice, based on his long experience with the West Virginia I-O Model, in the chorus of requests for the better regional data needed for improved regional economic models.

5 OUTPUT, INCOME, AND EMPLOYMENT INPUT-OUTPUT MULTIPLIERS*

Denise DiPasquale and Karen R. Polenske†

5.1 INTRODUCTION

When evaluating a public program, it is often important to know what effect a proposed policy will have on the output, income, or employment of the economy. The policy analyst may be interested in the answers to questions such as: How much additional income will be generated by a given policy or program? How many jobs will be created? How much additional output will be produced? Which industries in the economy will be affected most? Multiplier analysis is a tool that can help answer such questions. The

*The research reported in this paper is financed with funds from Grants No. OER-544-G-76-28 and No. OER-544-G-77-14 from the Economic Development Administration, U.S. Department of Commerce, to the Department of Urban Studies and Planning, Massachusetts Institute of Technology, Cambridge, Massachusetts. The authors take full responsibility for the conclusions, which are not necessarily those of the sponsoring agencies.

†The authors are, respectively, graduate student and Associate Professor of Urban and Regional Studies, Department of Urban Studies and Planning, Massachusetts Institute of Technology, Cambridge, Massachusetts. They gratefully acknowledge the assistance of Ananna Tse, who helped with the calculations; Ruth Rowan, with whom they discussed most of the material presented in the paper; Gordon King, who drew the figures; and Virginia Cox Randall, who assisted with the graphic preparations.

multiplier accounts not only for the effects of the spending outlined in the specific program, but also for the subsequent rounds of spending generated by the initial expenditures.

The Keynesian multiplier is traditionally thought of when considering the notion of a multiplier. This multiplier measures the total effect on the economy resulting from an exogenous change in investment, consumption expenditures, government spending, or foreign exports. It is a very aggregate measure that gives no indication of which industries or regions in the economy are most or least affected by the exogenous change. There are many instances where this detail is desired. For example, the policy under investigation may be an attempt to stimulate a particular sector of the economy. In this case, the policy analyst will be interested in how output, income, or employment in that particular sector will be affected by the proposed policy. Using an input-output model, this type of detailed multiplier may be derived.

A considerable amount of literature now exists concerning multiplier applications of the multiregional input-output (MRIO) model, including the publications of Faucett (1975), Golladay and Haveman (1977), Kim, Park, and Kwak (1975), and Hill (1975). But these authors did not specify the structure of the multipliers used. The purpose of this paper is to provide explicit details on the calculation and interpretation of multiregional output, employment, and income multipliers in theory, substantiated with actual data for the United States.

5.2 THE BASIC MRIO MODEL

The MRIO model provides a systematic framework for describing and analyzing not only the sales and purchases of all industries in the economy, but also the shipments to and from all regions. The model is a combination of a set of input-output tables for each of 51 regions (50 states plus the District of Columbia), and a set of regional trade-flow tables for each of 79 goods and services. The current input-output and trade-flow base data are for 1963, but state final demands have been estimated for 1970 and 1980, as well as for 1963, and a 1972 update of the base-year data is planned.

The model is a comprehensive, multipurpose tool that can be used for systematic studies of many regional economic policies. Numerous groups, including people working for federal and state government agencies, private consulting firms, and academic institutions, have used the MRIO data and model for a variety of regional and interregional policy analyses. Of the studies conducted by other groups, some of the most interesting are the Golladay and Haveman (1977) application of the model at the University of Wisconsin to evaluate the regional output, employment, and redistributional effects of a proposed federal income transfer policy; the employment analysis completed by Faucett (1975) for the Conrail Final System Plan; and the employment and water resource analysis made for the Arkansas River Project by Kim, Park, and Kwak (1975). At the MRIO research project, at the Massachusetts Institute of Technology, the model has been used for many different studies, among them Pucher's (1976) study to project rail freight shipments for five Midwestern railroads; a study by Rowan (1976) to make state employment projections for Massachusetts; and Polenske's (1976) examination of the interregional interactions between transportation and energy for nine regions. All of these studies were made using the primal form of the model. In current research, the model has been reformulated as a dual model to examine changes in regional prices (Polenske, 1976; Young, 1978). Because of the wide variation in the needs of users, the data and model were specifically designed for adaptability to different policy studies.

The fixed supply form of the static MRIO model is formulated using the following four assumptions:

1. *Constant technology coefficients.* No substitution among inputs is allowed to occur.
2. *Constant trade coefficients.* No substitution among supplying regions is allowed to occur. Thus, a region is assumed to continue supplying a given fraction of the consumption of another region over time. No empirical verification of this assumption has been possible because of the lack of data.
3. *Constant industrial shares.* Each industry in a given region is assumed to continue purchasing a fixed share of the total amount of a given good supplied to the region. Again, because of the lack of data, no empirical testing of this assumption has been made. By incorporating this assumption, however, the amount of data required to implement the model is drastically reduced.
4. *Excess capacity.* All producers and transportation facilities are assumed to be operating at less than full capacity.

To implement the system, a Chenery-Moses fixed-supply coefficient input-output model has been used. Since that model has been described in detail by Chenery (1953), Moses (1955), and Polenske (1972), only the basic

set of equations and the notations, to be used throughout the remainder of
this report, are presented here for n regions and m industries:

$$X = C(\hat{A}X + Y)$$
$$(I - C\hat{A})X = CY$$
$$X = (C^{-1} - \hat{A})^{-1}Y$$

where

$\hat{A}$ = matrix, nmxnm, of regional technical coefficients with each of the
n blocks located along the main diagonal and each block containing technical coefficients of the m industries for a specific region. Elements in all blocks off the main diagonal are zero.

C = matrix, nmxnm, with each of the diagonals of the nxm blocks
containing the trade coefficients, and with all off-diagonal elements in the nxm blocks equal to zero.

Y = vector, nmxl, of final demand, with each element representing
the amount of output that industry i must produce and sell
directly to final users in region h.

X = vector, nmxl, of total output.

I = identity matrix, nmxnm.

Given the base-year technical relationships that exist in the regional production processes, the interregional trade patterns, and a set of regional
final demands for the selected year, the total regional output of each industry and interregional shipments for that year can be calculated.

Two versions of the static input-output model will be discussed in this
report: open, and partially closed. In the open version all final demands are
treated exogenously; in the partially closed version, one or more of the final
demands (and the corresponding part of value added) are treated endogenously. In a model partially closed with respect to households, for example,
the personal consumption expenditures part of final demand, and the wages
and salaries portion of value added, will be treated as endogenous components of the model. The direct and indirect output requirements are
determined using the inverse matrix of the open model and a set of final
demands. In response to a given set of final demands, all industries produce
some output that is used as direct inputs in the production of the outputs.
But these inputs generate additional demands, so that more output must be
produced to fulfill those demand requirements; and this iterative procedure
continues as it converges towards zero. The total (direct and indirect)
requirements determined by this iterative process are assumed to be
obtained within a selected year.

The production of outputs to fulfill the given set of final demands also results in changes in income that, in turn, will lead to additional changes in final demand, say, personal consumption expenditures, touching off yet another series of reactions. The effects of these reactions on outputs, employment, and income are called induced changes, and they can be traced by partially closing the model. The direct, indirect, and induced-output requirements are determined using the inverse matrix of the partially closed model and a given set of final demands. For the partially closed model, one or more of the final demands, for example, personal consumption expenditures, are treated endogenously. The corresponding part of value added, in this case wages and salaries, must also become endogenous, its level now being determined by changes in the remaining exogenous final demands, whereas previously its level and composition were determined exogenously. Personal consumption expenditures and wages and salaries will now be referred to collectively as the household industry.

In the example just cited, personal consumption expenditures and wages and salaries become the $m + 1$ producing industry, with a technology represented by the expenditures pattern given in the personal consumption expenditures column of the MRIO table. Its output is distributed according to the amount of labor required by each industrial and final user in each region, as shown in the wages and salaries rows of the MRIO table. The inverse coefficients for this expanded matrix will now reflect, not only the direct and indirect output, employment, and income, but also the induced output, employment, and income required to fulfill the changed demands of households. Investment, foreign exports, or government expenditures could be made endogenous instead of households, depending upon the desired analysis.

5.3 MULTIPLIERS

The capabilities and usefulness of the Leontief matrix of direct and indirect coefficients, hereafter referred to as the Leontief inverse coefficients, are well known. Yet in the growing amount of literature on input-output multipliers, most authors neglect the Leontief inverse coefficients in their role as individual multipliers and concentrate instead on summary measures of them. This neglect has led to confusion as to what a multiplier is; how output, employment, and income multipliers are related; and with what data they should be combined. It has also obscured the rich detail of information that is available for planning purposes. The importance and usefulness of the individual inverse coefficients will become evident later.

For this study, the multiregional output, employment, or income multi-pliers are always combined with projected changes in final demand to determine the corresponding output, employment, or income effects of those expenditures; however, in most other studies, such as those by Moore and Petersen (1955), Hirsch (1959), and Miernyk (1965; 1967), the multipliers are divided by the direct income in the corresponding industry and region of demand, and are then combined with projected changes in direct income. The multiplier must always be established on a base that is consistent with the data by which it is to be multiplied. The base to be used will be partially determined by the ease of obtaining data projections for final demand, income, or some other variables. Most regional analysts have used direct income, perhaps because this measure is easily projected at the state level. Schaffer is one of the few analysts who does not divide by direct income; he specifies his multipliers in terms of changes in gross regional product, the same measure used in the present study (1976, pp. 60–61).

There are many different multipliers referred to in the literature. In this report, detailed definitions are given for output, employment, and income multipliers, in open and partially closed static multiregional and national (regional) input-output models. Four types of multipliers will be defined in the following sections: detailed, industry-specific, region-specific, and total.

5.3.1 Multiregional Output Multipliers

5.3.1.1 Detailed output multiplier. The total output multiplier is the one most frequently used in the literature. Like the industry-specific and region-specific, it is based on the multiregional detailed output multiplier. By definition, the multiregional detailed output multiplier for industries i and j and regions g and h is identical to the multiregional inverse coefficient for the same industries and regions. This multiplier is defined as:

$$XM_{ij}^{gh} \equiv d_{ij}^{gh} \qquad\qquad \begin{aligned} i,j &= 1, \ldots, m \\ g,h &= 1, \ldots, n \end{aligned} \qquad\qquad (5.1)$$

where

XM_{ij}^{gh} is the output multiplier for final demand in region h for commodity j and output in region g of commodity i.

d_{ij}^{gh} is the multiregional inverse coefficient for outputs, showing the amount of output generated by industry i located in region g to fulfill the final demand in region h for the products of industry j.

    i,j   are the *m* producing and purchasing industries, respectively (used as subscripts).

    g,h are the *n* shipping and receiving regions, respectively (used as superscripts).

    m   is the number of industries.

    n   is the number of regions.

When the detailed output multiplier is multiplied by the final demand (gross regional product) in region *h* for the output of industry *j*, the total amount of output generated by industry *i*, located in region *g*, to fulfill the change in a particular final demand is determined. For *m* industries and *n* regions, there are mnxmn such multipliers.[1]

The elements in the first column of table 5-1 are used as an example and are represented in bar-chart form in figure 5-1. For illustration, an inverse matrix, with the elements unspecified, based upon three industries and three regions, is shown schematically at the top of the page. The first column is enlarged below the matrix, with actual numbers from table 5-1, to illustrate the four different types of output multipliers. The enlarged column on the left, labeled "detailed," shows the separate elements in the inverse matrix, with the divisions based upon the size of each individual output multiplier, taken from table 5-1.

According to these data, a $1 increase in demand for the output of Industry 1, Agriculture & mining, in the North will generate only $0.734 of agriculture and mining output in the North, $0.190 of manufacturing and construction output in the North, and $0.178 of services output in the North. Output will also be produced in other regions as a result of the particular demand in the North — $0.332 of agriculture and mining output, $0.081 of manufacturing and construction output, and $0.083 of services output will be contributed by the South, while $0.249 of agriculture and mining output, $0.052 of manufacturing and construction output, and $0.067 of services output will be contributed by the West. In sum, a $1 increase in demand for agriculture and mining in the North will increase total output of all industries in all regions throughout the country by $1.966 — which is the sum of all elements in the detailed bar chart. It is represented by the total bar chart at the right of figure 5-1. The $1.966 output generated is almost double the original $1 demand.

5.3.1.2 Industry-specific output multiplier. For some analyses, the aggregate output of a specific industry generated by a change in final demand in a

Table 5-1. Multiregional detailed output multipliers: open model

	North			South			West		
	1 Agri. mining	2 Constr. mfg.	3 Serv.	1 Agri. mining	2 Constr. mfg.	3 Serv.	1 Agri. mining	2 Constr. mfg.	3 Serv.
1 Agr., mining	0.734	0.055	0.010	0.148	0.036	0.006	0.059	0.027	0.004
N2 Construc., mfg.	0.190	1.338	0.118	0.119	0.540	0.064	0.101	0.491	0.056
3 Services	0.178	0.213	1.146	0.086	0.118	0.215	0.061	0.101	0.138
1 Agr., mining	0.332	0.045	0.007	0.905	0.100	0.016	0.136	0.037	0.006
S2 Construc., mfg.	0.081	0.230	0.025	0.146	0.989	0.079	0.051	0.182	0.023
3 Services	0.083	0.050	0.068	0.188	0.151	0.979	0.051	0.046	0.084
1 Agr., mining	0.249	0.036	0.006	0.199	0.043	0.007	1.199	0.125	0.019
W2 Construc., mfg.	0.052	0.128	0.016	0.048	0.143	0.019	0.153	0.971	0.081
3 Services	0.067	0.039	0.065	0.060	0.044	0.083	0.247	0.167	1.056
Total*	1.966	2.134	1.463	1.898	2.164	1.469	2.058	2.147	1.468

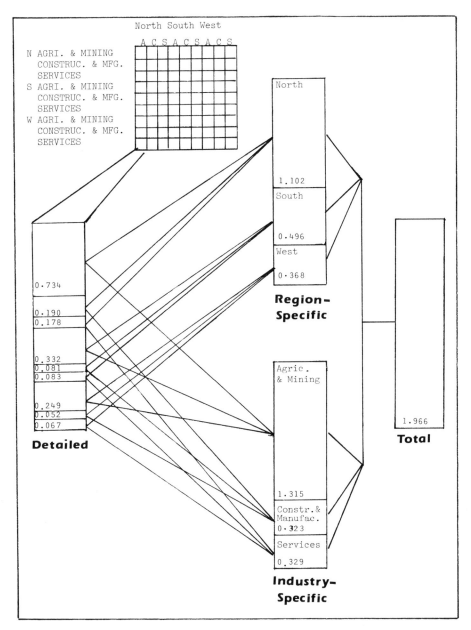

Figure 5-1.   Multiregional output multipliers for agriculture and mining in the North—
open model.

particular region may be of interest. This multiplier will be called the multi-regional industry-specific output multiplier, which is defined as:

$$XM_{ij}^{oh} = \sum_{g=1}^{n} d_{ij}^{gh} \qquad\qquad \begin{matrix} i,j = 1, \ldots, m \\ h = 1, \ldots, n \end{matrix} \qquad\qquad (5.2)$$

where all elements are defined as in equation (5.1), and o represents a summation over all regions.

This multiplier is obtained by summing all elements in a column (for a specific industry and region) of the MRIO inverse that refer to a specific industry. When it is multiplied by the final demand in region h for the output of industry j, the total amount of output generated by industry i in all regions to fulfill that particular final demand is determined. Thus, the region in which the output is generated is not given, but the specific industry generating the output is known; hence the name industry-specific. In the example of the three-industry, three-region, (open) model given in figure 5–1, there are three industry-specific multipliers for the agriculture and mining industry in the North: one for Industry 1 of $1.315; on for Industry 2 of $0.323; and one for Industry 3 of $0.329 — each formed by summing the relevant detailed output multipliers for the three regions.

The North does not produce all the agriculture and mining output required to fulfill the demand for that product in the North; some of the output is produced in the South or the West and shipped to the North. The industry-specific multiplier of 1.315 represents a summation of the multipliers from the three regions and shows the total amount of agricultural and mining output produced throughout the country to fulfill the $1 of demand for the product in the North. It is larger than 1 for the same reason that the national detailed output multipliers on the diagonal of the national inverse matrix are larger than 1; that is, because $1 of its output must be produced just to fulfill the $1 of demand. The remaining $0.315 represents the direct and indirect requirements to produce the output.

There are twenty-seven industry-specific multipliers for the open model (three for each of the nine columns in table 5–1) and forty-eight for the partially closed model (four for each of the twelve columns in table 5–2). These are given in tables 5–3 and 5–4. In general, there will be nxm^2 multiregional industry-specific multipliers. For these multipliers, one of the regional dimensions of the multiregional detailed output multiplier is withheld: that is, the region in which the output is being produced. These multipliers are used when a policy analyst or planner needs to know how much output will be generated by each industry in the country, per unit change in demand for the output of an industry in a specific region.

5.3.1.3 Region-specific output multiplier. A related summary output multiplier measure is the multiregional region-specific output multiplier. In

Table 5-2. Multiregional detailed output multipliers: partially closed model

	North				South				West			
	1 Agri. mining	2 Constr. mfg.	3 Serv.	4 P.C.E.	1 Agri. mining	2 Constr. mfg.	3 Serv.	4 P.C.E.	1 Agri. mining	2 Constr. mfg.	3 Serv.	4 P.C.E.
N 1 Agr., mining	0.746	0.079	0.031	0.056	0.158	0.053	0.020	0.033	0.068	0.042	0.016	0.026
N 2 Construc., mfg.	0.367	1.718	0.444	0.870	0.258	0.781	0.264	0.441	0.231	0.732	0.247	0.411
N 3 Services	0.411	0.733	1.617	1.283	0.246	0.427	0.433	0.423	0.196	0.389	0.323	0.340
N 4 Wage-salary	0.255	0.610	0.563	1.577	0.141	0.305	0.185	0.224	0.114	0.282	0.150	0.193
S 1 Agr., mining	0.346	0.067	0.025	0.043	0.923	0.129	0.045	0.086	0.148	0.056	0.022	0.035
S 2 Construc., mfg.	0.153	0.327	0.104	0.179	0.258	1.172	0.263	0.576	0.109	0.271	0.099	0.157
S 3 Services	0.176	0.164	0.144	0.149	0.357	0.399	1.271	0.940	0.121	0.153	0.167	0.160
S 4 Wage-salary	0.108	0.110	0.061	0.077	0.231	0.332	0.403	1.387	0.067	0.096	0.066	0.076
W 1 Agr., mining	0.262	0.056	0.022	0.036	0.212	0.062	0.024	0.040	1.224	0.162	0.059	0.109
W 2 Construc., mfg.	0.105	0.196	0.072	0.113	0.098	0.211	0.079	0.124	0.276	1.161	0.284	0.583
W 3 Services	0.150	0.141	0.140	0.139	0.139	0.149	0.166	0.158	0.466	0.481	1.429	1.075
W 4 Wage-salary	0.085	0.087	0.058	0.067	0.077	0.093	0.067	0.076	0.284	0.398	0.487	1.457
Total*	3.165	4.288	3.282	4.591	3.097	4.113	3.222	4.506	3.301	4.222	3.348	4.622

Table 5-3. Multiregional industry-specific and region-specific output multipliers: open model

Industry Specific

	North			South			West		
	1 Agri. mining	2 Constr. mfg.	3 Serv.	1 Agri. mining	2 Constr. mg.	3 Serv.	1 Agri. mining	2 Constr. mfg.	3 Serv.
1 Agr., mining	1.315	0.136	0.024	1.251	0.178	0.029	1.395	0.189	0.029
2 Construc., mfg.	0.323	1.696	0.160	0.312	1.672	0.163	0.305	1.644	0.160
3 Services	0.329	0.303	1.279	0.335	0.313	1.278	0.359	0.315	1.278
Total*	1.966	2.134	1.463	1.898	2.164	1.469	2.058	2.147	1.468

Region Specific

	North			South			West		
	1 Agri. mining	2 Constr. mfg.	3 Serv.	1 Agri. mining	2 Constr. mfg.	3 Serv.	1 Agri. mining	2 Constr. mfg.	3 Serv.
1 North	1.102	1.606	1.274	0.353	0.693	0.285	0.221	0.619	0.198
2 South	0.496	0.325	0.101	1.238	1.240	1.075	0.238	0.265	0.133
3 West	0.368	0.204	0.088	0.307	0.230	0.109	1.599	1.263	1.156
Total*	1.966	2.134	1.463	1.898	2.164	1.469	2.058	2.147	1.468

Table 5–4. Multiregional industry-specific and region-specific output multipliers: partially closed model

Industry Specific

| | North | | | | South | | | | West | | | |
	1 Agri. mining	2 Constr. mfg.	3 Serv.	4 P.C.E.	1 Agri. mining	2 Constr. mfg.	3 Serv.	4 P.C.E.	1 Agri. mining	2 Constr. mfg.	3 Serv.	4 P.C.E.
1 Agr., mining	1.354	0.202	0.079	0.135	1.293	0.244	0.089	0.159	1.439	0.260	0.097	0.170
2 Construc., mfg.	0.625	2.241	0.620	1.162	0.615	2.165	0.606	1.140	0.616	2.164	0.630	1.152
3 Services	0.737	1.038	1.901	1.571	0.741	0.975	1.871	1.520	0.782	1.022	1.919	1.575
4 Wage-salary	0.449	0.807	0.682	1.722	0.449	0.730	0.656	1.687	0.464	0.776	0.702	1.726
Total*	3.165	4.288	3.282	4.591	3.097	4.113	3.222	4.506	3.301	4.222	3.348	4.622

Region Specific

| | North | | | | South | | | | West | | | |
	1 Agri. mining	2 Constr. mfg.	3 Serv.	4 P.C.E.	1 Agri. mining	2 Constr. mfg.	3 Serv.	4 P.C.E.	1 Agri. mining	2 Constr. mfg.	3 Serv.	4 P.C.E.
1 North	1.779	3.140	2.656	3.785	0.802	1.566	0.903	1.121	0.608	1.445	0.735	0.970
2 South	0.783	0.669	0.334	0.449	1.769	2.032	1.983	2.989	0.443	0.575	0.354	0.428
3 West	0.602	0.480	0.292	0.356	0.526	0.515	0.336	0.397	2.249	2.201	2.259	3.223
Total*	3.165	4.288	3.282	4.591	3.097	4.113	3.222	4.506	3.301	4.222	3.348	4.622

this case, one of the industry dimensions of the multiregional detailed output multiplier, the industry producing the output, is withheld; but now the region in which the output is produced is known — hence the name region-specific. It is defined as:

$$XM_{oj}^{gh} = \sum_{i=1}^{m} d_{ij}^{gh} \qquad\qquad \begin{aligned} j &= 1, \ldots, m \\ g,h &= 1, \ldots, n \end{aligned} \qquad (5.3)$$

where all elements are defined as in equation (5.1), and o represents a summation over all industries.

The multiplier is obtained by summing all the elements in a column-block of the MRIO inverse matrix, where each column is blocked according to regions. (The blocking is illustrated in tables 5-1 and 5-2.) When it is multiplied by the final demand in region h for the output of industry j, the total amount of output, generated by all industries in a particular region in order to fulfill that particular final demand, is determined. In the example of the three-industry, three-region, (open) model given in figure 5-1, there are three region-specific multipliers for the agriculture and mining industry in the North: one for Region 1 of $1.102; one for Region 2 of $0.496; and one for Region 3 of $0.368; each is formed by summing the relevant detailed output multipliers in the corresponding column-block of the inverse (table 5-1) for the three industries in each region.

There are twenty-seven region-specific multipliers for the open model (three for each of the nine columns in table 5-1), and thirty-six for the partially closed model (three for each of the twelve columns in table 5-2). These are given in tables 5-3 and 5-4. In general, there will be mxn^2 multiregional region-specific multipliers. The industry-specific and region-specific summary multipliers may be especially useful to analysts and planners interested in the impacts on regional output of changes in the composition and level of gross regional product.

5.3.1.4 Total output multiplier. An even more aggregate summary measure of output multipliers can now be determined. For this multiplier, both the regional and industrial origin of output are withheld; only the region and industry where the demand originates are known. This will be called the multiregional total output multiplier. It is defined as:

$$\begin{aligned} XM_j^h &= \sum_{i=1}^{m} XM_{ij}^{oh} = \sum_{g=1}^{n} XM_{oj}^{gh} \\ &= \sum_{i=1}^{m} \sum_{g=1}^{n} d_{ij}^{gh} \qquad\qquad \begin{aligned} j &= 1, \ldots, m \\ h &= 1, \ldots, n \end{aligned} \qquad (5.4) \end{aligned}$$

where all elements are as defined in equations (5.1), (5.2), and (5.3).

When this figure is multiplied by the final demand in region h for the output of industry j, the total amount of output, generated by all industries in all regions to fulfill that particular final demand, is determined. It is obtained by adding either the m industry-specific output multipliers, or the n region-specific output multipliers, or the mn detailed output multipliers for industry j in region h. In other words, it is the sum of the elements in a column of the inverse matrix of coefficients — in relation to figure 5-1, the value 1.966. The multiregional total output multipliers for all industries for the open and partially closed models are the sums shown at the bottom of tables 5-1 and 5-2, respectively. For a total of m industries and n regions, there are mn multiregional total output multipliers. These multipliers are provided for each industry in each region where demand is originating, but no information is provided concerning either the industry or region producing the output — and this detail is often of critical importance to planners.

From the above discussion, the immense amount of detail provided by multiregional multipliers is evident. Because they are based on the output multipliers, the other frequently used multipliers — employment and income — can be easily explained.

5.3.2 Open Model Employment and Income Multipliers

Underlying all MRIO employment and income multiplier calculations are the production structures in, and transportation networks among, regions. Differences between industries and between regions in employment multipliers, for example, are then only partly the result of variations in employment-to-output ratios. Shifts in interindustry and interregional structures of production and transportation, respectively, will also affect the size of the multiplier. The same holds for income, energy, and other MRIO multipliers.

Corresponding to each of the six output multipliers specified above for the open model is an employment and income multiplier, each based upon the same set of inverse coefficient relationships. The inverse coefficients are now combined with either an employment-to-output ratio or an income-to-output ratio. These ratios are shown in table 5-5. The calculation is done as follows. According to the procedure now well established in the national employment estimations made by the U.S. Bureau of Labor Statistics (1975), each element in a row of the inverse matrix is multiplied by the employment-to-output (income-to-output) ratio for the particular industry represented by the row. The same procedure is used at the multiregional level, with the industries now being differentiated by the region, as well as the industry, in which the output is produced.

Table 5–5. Multiregional employment-to-output and income-to-output ratios

	Employment-to-output ratios	Income-to-output ratios
1 Agr., mining	23,379	0.072
2 Construc., mfg.	38,088	0.229
N 3 Services	60,931	0.281
4 Wages & salaries	7,890	0.008
1 Agr., mining	43,103	0.092
2 Construc., mfg.	37,410	0.176
S 3 Services	68,607	0.273
4 Wages & salaries	8,293	0.016
1 Agr., mining	24,301	0.072
2 Construc., mfg.	32,881	0.208
W 3 Services	63,606	0.293
4 Wages & salaries	4,325	0.008
Total	36,662	0.172

For the income multipliers an income-to-output ratio is used, and this happens to be already present in the matrix of direct input coefficients as the household industry row for the wages and salaries paid to labor. This household coefficient, in a particular column of the multiregional direct input coefficient matrix, is obtained by dividing the wages and salaries in industry i in region g by the corresponding output of industry i in region g.

The specific equations for the multiregional detailed employment and income multipliers are:

$$\text{EM}_{ij}^{gh} = d_{ij}^{gh} * \frac{e_{io}^{go}}{x_{io}^{go}} \qquad \begin{array}{l} i,j = 1, \ldots, m \\ g,h = 1, \ldots, n \end{array} \qquad (5.5\text{a})$$

$$\text{WM}_{ij}^{gh} = d_{ij}^{gh} * \frac{x_{wi}^{go}}{x_{io}^{go}} \qquad \begin{array}{l} i,j = 1, \ldots, m \\ g,h = 1, \ldots, n \end{array} \qquad (5.5\text{b})$$

where

EM_{ij}^{gh} is the employment multiplier for final demand in region h for commodity j and employment in region g for commodity i.

WM_{ij}^{gh} is the income (wage and salary) multiplier for final demand in region h for commodity j and income in region g for commodity i.

d_{ij}^{gh} is the multiregional inverse coefficient for outputs, showing the amount of output generated by industry i in region g to fulfill the final demand in region h for the products of industry j.

e_{io}^{go} is the total employment required to produce commodity i in region g.

x_{io}^{go} is the total output of commodity i in region g.

x_{wi}^{go} is the total income (wages and salaries) paid to produce commodity i in region g.

From these equations it can be seen that the base of each of the multipliers is the multiregional direct and indirect (output) coefficient. The output multiplier relationship is adjusted in each case by either the employment-to-output or income-to-output ratio. Actual detailed employment and income multipliers for the MRIO open model are shown in tables 5–6 and 5–7.

The multiregional employment and income multipliers contain considerable industrial and regional detail, as there is a separate multiplier for each industry in each region. As was the case for output multipliers, the greatest amount of information on employment and income impacts is determined through the use of the detailed multipliers, and the least determined through the use of the total multipliers.

5.3.3 Output, Employment, and Income Multipliers for the Partially Closed Model

The four basic types of multiregional multipliers (detailed, industry-specific, region-specific, and total) all condense into a single number the several rounds of reactions that occur in output, employment, and income over a finite time period. In the static model, the total reaction to an increase or decrease of final demand is assumed to occur within the given year. However, as mentioned earlier, the resulting changes in income will lead to additional changes in final demand, touching off yet another series of reactions. These induced changes are reflected in the inverse coefficients for the partially closed model. Thus, each inverse coefficient (detailed multiplier) in the partially closed model will be as large as or larger than the corresponding coefficient (detailed multiplier) in the open model, which can be cross-checked by comparing the corresponding coefficients in tables 5–1 and 5–2 (or tables 5–6 and 5–8, or tables 5–7 and 5–9). Each of the remaining three types of multipliers will likewise be larger for the partially closed model than for the open model.

5.3.3.1 Output multipliers. The three-region, three-industry data will again be used to illustrate the effect numerically. The detailed output multipliers (inverse coefficients) for the partially closed model are shown in the

Table 5-6. Multiregional detailed employment multipliers: open model

	North			South			West		
	1 Agri. mining	2 Constr. mfg.	3 Serv.	1 Agri. mining	2 Constr. mfg.	3 Serv.	1 Agri. mining	2 Constr. mfg.	3 Serv.
N 1 Agr., mining	17165	1280	244	3456	831	137	1388	622	94
2 Construc., mfg.	7225	50944	4494	4515	20564	2451	3832	18709	2138
3 Services	19861	13000	69803	5270	7167	13092	3722	6175	8424
S 1 Agr., mining	14314	1935	319	39009	4316	702	5872	1605	253
2 Construc., mfg.	3017	8592	952	5452	37013	2973	1908	6794	869
3 Services	5693	3461	4666	12883	10357	67196	3487	3168	5774
W 1 Agr., mining	6041	885	153	4829	1039	172	29142	3030	474
2 Construc., mfg.	1718	4224	540	1564	4702	622	5042	31933	2664
3 Services	4303	2481	4179	3856	2829	5316	15764	10681	67469
Total*	70338	86803	85349	80835	88817	92661	70157	82715	88158

Table 5-7. Multiregional detailed income multipliers: open model

	North			South			West		
	1 Agri. mining	2 Constr. mfg.	3 Serv.	1 Agri. mining	2 Constr. mfg.	3 Serv.	1 Agri. mining	2 Constr. mfg.	3 Serv.
1 Agr., mining	0.053	0.004	0.001	0.011	0.003	0.000	0.004	0.002	0.000
N 2 Construc., mfg.	0.043	0.306	0.027	0.027	0.124	0.015	0.023	0.112	0.013
3 Services	0.050	0.060	0.322	0.024	0.033	0.060	0.017	0.028	0.039
1 Agr., mining	0.031	0.004	0.001	0.003	0.009	0.001	0.013	0.003	0.001
S 2 Construc., mfg.	0.014	0.040	0.004	0.026	0.174	0.014	0.009	0.032	0.004
3 Services	0.023	0.014	0.019	0.051	0.041	0.267	0.014	0.013	0.023
1 Agr., mining	0.018	0.003	0.000	0.014	0.003	0.001	0.086	0.009	0.001
W 2 Construc., mfg.	0.011	0.027	0.003	0.010	0.030	0.004	0.032	0.202	0.017
3 Services	0.020	0.011	0.019	0.018	0.013	0.024	0.072	0.049	0.307
Total*	0.262	0.469	0.308	0.264	0.430	0.387	0.270	0.451	0.407

Table 5-8. Multiregional detailed employment multipliers: partially closed model

	North				South				West			
	1 Agri. mining	2 Constr. mfg.	3 Serv.	4 P.C.E.	1 Agri. mining	2 Constr. mfg.	3 Serv.	4 P.C.E.	1 Agri. mining	2 Constr. mfg.	3 Serv.	4 P.C.E.
N 1 Agr., mining	17440	1846	736	1308	3684	1231	469	773	1584	991	378	601
2 Construc., mfg.	13976	65402	16909	33121	9831	29752	10068	16782	8794	27878	9396	15657
3 Services	25028	44646	98541	78172	14989	26006	26399	25775	11929	23686	19660	20738
4 Wage-salary	2012	4815	4444	12441	1110	2409	1462	1768	897	2228	1181	1525
S 1 Agri., mining	14904	2870	1085	1847	39794	5572	1948	3716	6364	2420	943	1513
2 Construc., mfg.	5727	12243	3909	6710	9654	43856	9835	21536	4068	10134	3713	5891
3 Services	12079	11285	9867	10256	24461	27362	87228	64457	8267	10464	11466	10957
4 Wage-salary	899	914	505	642	1918	2751	3346	11504	552	705	548	627
W 1 Agri., mining	6362	1361	543	885	5147	1507	584	962	29731	3033	1423	2645
2 Construc., mfg.	3455	6445	2356	3728	3288	6940	2582	4074	9084	38168	9348	19176
3 Services	9590	9006	8942	8863	8867	9527	10618	10082	29746	30716	91312	68659
4 Wage-salary	369	376	251	292	333	402	291	327	1229	1720	2105	6300
Total*	111841	161226	148088	158266	123026	157315	154831	161757	112246	153132	151472	154289

Table 5-9. Multiregional detailed income multipliers: partially closed model

| | | North | | | | South | | | | West | | |
		1 Agri. mining	2 Constr. mfg.	3 Serv.	4 P.C.E.	1 Agri. mining	2 Constr. mfg.	3 Serv.	4 P.C.E.	1 Agri. mining	2 Constr. mfg.	3 Serv.	4 P.C.E.
N	1 Agr., mining	0.054	0.006	0.002	0.004	0.011	0.004	0.001	0.002	0.005	0.003	0.001	0.002
	2 Construc., mfg.	0.084	0.393	0.102	0.199	0.059	0.179	0.061	0.101	0.053	0.168	0.056	0.094
	3 Services	0.115	0.206	0.454	0.361	0.069	0.120	0.122	0.119	0.055	0.109	0.091	0.096
	4 Wage-salary	0.002	0.005	0.005	0.013	0.001	0.002	0.001	0.002	0.001	0.002	0.001	0.002
S	1 Agr., mining	0.032	0.006	0.002	0.004	0.085	0.012	0.004	0.008	0.014	0.005	0.002	0.003
	2 Construc., mfg.	0.027	0.058	0.018	0.032	0.045	0.206	0.046	0.101	0.019	0.048	0.017	0.028
	3 Services	0.048	0.045	0.039	0.041	0.097	0.109	0.347	0.256	0.033	0.042	0.046	0.044
	4 Wage-salary	0.002	0.002	0.001	0.001	0.004	0.005	0.006	0.022	0.001	0.002	0.001	0.001
W	1 Agr., mining	0.019	0.004	0.002	0.003	0.015	0.004	0.002	0.003	0.088	0.012	0.004	0.008
	2 Construc., mfg.	0.022	0.041	0.015	0.024	0.020	0.044	0.016	0.026	0.057	0.241	0.059	0.121
	3 Services	0.044	0.041	0.041	0.041	0.041	0.044	0.049	0.046	0.136	0.141	0.419	0.315
	4 Wage-salary	0.001	0.001	0.000	0.001	0.001	0.001	0.001	0.001	0.002	0.003	0.004	0.012
	Total**	0.449	0.807	0.682	0.721	0.449	0.730	0.656	0.687	0.465	0.775	0.702	0.725

first column of table 5-2. These have been reproduced in bar-chart form in figure 5-2. The first element indicates that a $1 increase in final demand in the North for the output of Industry 1, Agriculture & mining, generates $0.746 of output by the agriculture and mining industry in the North. The second element provides the total amount of output ($0.367) generated in the North in Industry 2, Construction & manufacturing, as a result of the same $1 increase in final demand; and the third element provides the total amount of output ($0.411) generated in the North in Industry 3, Services. The fourth element is especially important, because it gives the total amount of wages and salaries generated in all the industries in the North — in this case, $0.255. The wages and salaries generated in other regions by the final demand in the North for the output of agriculture and mining, can be determined by looking at the eighth and twelfth elements in the column— $0.108 in wages and salaries is generated in the South, and $0.085 in the West.

5.3.3.2 Income multipliers. The detailed output multipliers for the household industry can easily be shown to be identical to the region-specific income multipliers for the same industry in the particular region (North, South, or West). To do this, detailed income multipliers are first formed. As in the case of the open model, detailed income multipliers are formed by multiplying the inverse coefficient (output multiplier) by the income-to-output ratio for each industry. (Income-to-output ratios are given in table 5-5.) If this is done for the first four industries in the first column, the following results are obtained:

Industry	Income-to-output ratio		Inverse coefficient		Detailed income multiplier
Agriculture & mining	0.072	×	0.746	=	0.054
Construction & manufacturing	0.229	×	0.367	=	0.084
Services	0.281	×	0.411	=	0.115
Wages & salaries	0.008	×	0.255	=	0.002
Region-specific (North) income multiplier					0.255

Each of the elements in the last column above is a detailed income multiplier for the partially closed model; these multipliers are shown for all industries and regions in table 5-9, and given in bar-chart form for the first column in figure 5-3. The total, 0.255, is the region-specific income multiplier for Region 1, North, and is identical (except for rounding) to the detailed output

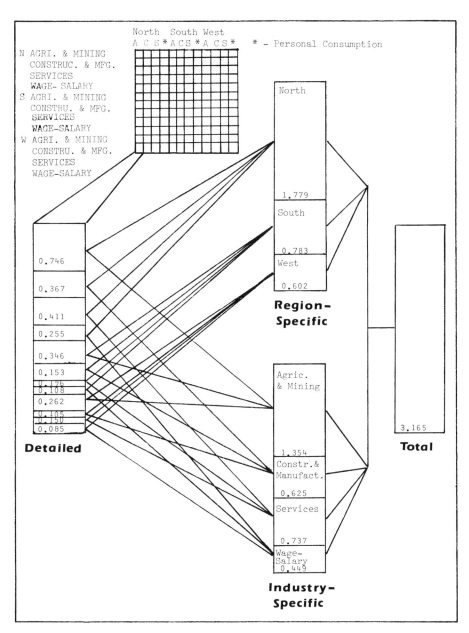

Figure 5-2.   Multiregional output multipliers for agriculture and mining in the North—partially closed model.

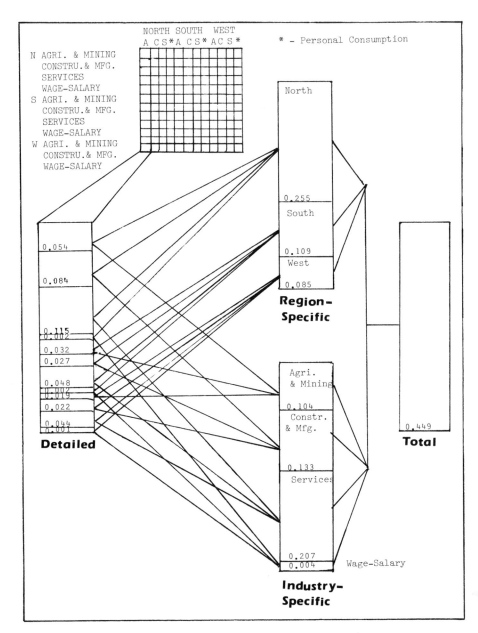

Figure 5-3. Multiregional income multipliers for agriculture and mining in the North—partially closed model.

multiplier 0.255 shown in the direct and indirect (output) coefficient column and the wage and salary row. The latter multiplier indicates the total of all income generated in Region 1 per dollar of final demand for agriculture & mining products in the North. The last column in the above table shows the industrial breakdown of the total regional income generated.

The region-specific income multipliers for all industries are given in table 5–10. The important point is that these region-specific income multipliers for the wages and salaries industry are identical to the detailed output multipliers for the household industry in the partially closed model, as given in the three wages and salaries rows in the first column of table 5–2.

Industry-specific income multipliers can also be calculated. These multipliers show the total amount of income generated in a given industry as a result of a $1 change in demand in a given industry. For example, if the demand for the output of Industry 1, Agriculture & mining, changes by $1, the total income generated in, say, the same industry, can be obtained by multiplying the three inverse coefficients (detailed output multipliers) for agriculture and mining in the first column of table 5–2 by their respective direct income coefficients, and then summing, as follows:

Region	Income-to-output ratio		Inverse coefficient		Detailed income multiplier
North	0.072	×	0.746	=	0.054
South	0.092	×	0.346	=	0.032
West	0.072	×	0.262	=	0.019
Industry-specific (agriculture & mining) income multiplier					0.104

As a result of the $1 increase in final demand for agriculture and mining in the North, 0.105 income is generated by the agriculture and mining industry throughout the nation (shown also in the industry-specific income multipliers in table 5–10).

5.3.3.3 Employment multipliers. The formulation of the employment multipliers for the partially closed model is analogous to that just illustrated for the income multipliers. In this case, the inverse coefficients of the partially closed model, which represent the output generated by a $1 change in demand, are multiplied by the respective employment-to-output ratios. This product gives the amount of employment generated per unit of output. (Employment-to-output ratios are given in table 5–5.) For example, in 1963,

Table 5-10. Multiregional industry-specific and region-specific income multipliers: partially closed model

Industry specific

| | North | | | | South | | | | West | | | |
	1 Agri. mining	2 Constr. mfg.	3 Serv.	4 P.C.E.	1 Agri. mining	2 Constr. mfg.	3 Serv.	4 P.C.E.	1 Agri. mining	2 Constr. mfg.	3 Serv.	4 P.C.E.
1 Agr., mining	0.104	0.016	0.006	0.011	0.112	0.020	0.007	0.013	0.107	0.020	0.007	0.013
2 Construc., mfg.	0.133	0.492	0.135	0.254	0.125	0.429	0.123	0.228	0.129	0.457	0.133	0.243
3 Services	0.207	0.292	0.535	0.442	0.207	0.273	0.518	0.422	0.224	0.292	0.555	0.454
4 Wage-salary	0.004	0.007	0.006	0.014	0.005	0.008	0.008	0.025	0.004	0.007	0.006	0.014
Total*	0.449	0.807	0.682	0.721	0.449	0.730	0.656	0.687	0.465	0.775	0.702	0.725

Region specific

| | North | | | | South | | | | West | | | |
	1 Agri. mining	2 Constr. mfg.	3 Serv.	4 P.C.E.	1 Agri. mining	2 Constr. mfg.	3 Serv.	4 P.C.E.	1 Agri. mining	2 Constr. mfg.	3 Serv.	4 P.C.E.
1 North	0.255	0.610	0.563	0.576	0.141	0.305	0.185	0.224	0.114	0.282	0.150	0.193
2 South	0.109	0.110	0.061	0.078	0.231	0.332	0.404	0.388	0.067	0.096	0.066	0.076
3 West	0.085	0.087	0.058	0.067	0.077	0.093	0.067	0.075	0.284	0.397	0.486	0.456
Total*	0.449	0.807	0.682	0.721	0.449	0.730	0.656	0.687	0.465	0.775	0.702	0.725

total employment for the first industry was 432,752 and total output was $18.51 billion, giving an employment-to-output ratio of 432,752/18.51, or 23,379, indicating that, for each $1 billion increase in output of agriculture and mining, employment will increase by 23,379 laborers. The detailed and industry-specific employment multipliers for agriculture and mining for the partially closed model are calculated as follows:

Region	Employ-ment-to-output ratio		Inverse coefficient		Detailed employ-ment multiplier
North	23,379	×	0.746	=	17,440
South	43,103	×	0.346	=	14,904
West	24,301	×	0.262	=	6,362
Industry-specific (Agriculture & mining) employment multiplier					38,706

The employment-to-output ratio is multiplied by the inverse coefficient to obtain the detailed employment multiplier; then the detailed multipliers for each of the three regions are summed to obtain the industry-specific — in this case, Agriculture & mining — employment multiplier. As a result of an increased $1 billion demand for agriculture and mining in the North, 38,706 jobs are generated in the agriculture and mining industry in the country. The detailed employment multipliers for the partially closed model are given in table 5–8.

As with the previous multipliers, region-specific multipliers may also be calculated. Again using the change in demand for agriculture and mining in the North, the following multipliers are determined:

Industry	Employ-ment-to-output ratio		Inverse coefficient		Employ-ment multiplier
Agriculture & mining	23,379	×	0.746	=	17,440
Construction & manufacturing	38,088	×	0.367	=	13,976
Services	60,931	×	0.411	=	25,028
Wages & salaries	7,890	×	0.255	=	2,012
Region-specific (North) employment multiplier					58,455

As a result of the $1 billion increase in demand for agriculture and mining in the North, employment generated by all industries in the North will increase by 58,456 laborers. The total multiplier in each of the cases mentioned in this report can be obtained either by summing the respective column of the detailed multiplier table, by summing the n region-specific multipliers for that industry and region, or by summing the m industry-specific multipliers for that industry and region.

5.4 CONCLUSION

By specifying multipliers in complete regional and industrial detail, it is possible to show the relationships among the multiregional and national input-output multipliers. The national detailed, industry-specific, region-specific, and total multipliers are weighted (by final demand) sums of the inverse of the direct input coefficients for each region, divided by the respective national final demand. Region-to-region differences among multipliers are obviously the result of the variations in technological, product-mix, and transportation structures that exist in each region. Variations in the national output multipliers therefore reflect differences in these factors from one industry to another.

In contrast to national output multipliers, the multiregional detailed output multipliers show in which industry and region the demand is located, as well as the industry and region in which the output is generated. As shown in table 5-1 for the open MRIO model, all of the multipliers, including those on the diagonal, are less than 1.0. Part of the importance for policy analyses of the multiregional, as compared with national, multipliers now becomes evident. In the national Leontief inverse for the open, static model, a $1 increase in final demand (GNP) for the output of industry i will always generate at least $1 of output by industry i, because $1 must be sold to final users (all elements on the diagonal of the national Leontief inverse are always 1.0 or greater than 1.0). This national detailed output multiplier does not, however, indicate in which region the output will be produced to fulfill the demand requirement. It becomes obvious that, if the national detailed intraindustry multiplier is larger than 1 but less than 2, each of the three regions in the present example cannot produce $1 of output of industry i; therefore, some, if not all, of the multiregional detailed multipliers for the open model will be less than 1.

The immense amount of information provided by the detailed MRIO output, employment, or income multipliers is valuable for those regional planners who need to know in which industries and regions output, employment, or income changes will occur. The usefulness of these detailed MRIO multipliers for policy analyses and planning is evident; however, the point should be stressed. Knowledge of the industry and region in which the output changes will occur can also be used — by transportation planners, to determine changes in transportation networks, rolling stock, and other equipment required to meet the shifts in industrial and regional production; by investment planners, to designate industries and regions where capital replacement or expansion is needed; by energy planners, to determine the impacts that production, transportation, and investment changes will have on energy demands; and by various other types of planners.

In contrast to the detailed regional (national) multipliers, from which only one summary measure can be derived, the multiregional detailed multipliers are the basis for three summary measures. Each of these multiregional summary measures provides regional information on impacts which cannot be obtained from the national detailed or total multipliers. The multiregional detailed multipliers also illustrate very well the import and export leakages that occur as the analysis is taken from the national to the multiregional level.

If some other kind of multiplier relationship were desired, such as an energy or investment multiplier, the same basic type of adjustment would be required. In the case of the investment relationship, the well-known accelerator principle becomes involved. This research can now be extended to show multiplier relationships other than those of output, employment, and income specified here.

NOTE

1. The term *detailed* in this report refers to the fact that for the national, regional, or multiregional multipliers, industrial detail is provided for both the producing industry and the industry where the demand is being generated, and for the multiregional multiplier the shipping and purchasing regions are specified as well. The multiregional output multipliers defined in this study are always combined with changes in the final demand — that is, gross regional product.

6 A GENERALIZED SPECIFICATION OF REGIONAL LABOR MARKETS

Donald Ratajczak*

6.1 INTRODUCTION

In recent years, regional models have advanced significantly beyond a statistical reallocation of national behavior. Differences in regional behavior are now explained by more than differences in the income responsiveness of local industries to national conditions and the regional composition of industries. The relative competitiveness of local industries in national markets is also being used in model construction.[1] Differential impacts of national policy variables, which have long been utilized, are being augmented by the impacts of many local policy variables.[2] Some concepts discussed in the literature on regional economics, such as economic base analysis,[3] the emphasis on interregional trade,[4] and interregional factor flows, especially population migration,[5] have found their way into specifications of regional econometric models. However, an underlying behavioral model that explains why regional growth rates differ and why some regional business cycles differ from national fluctuations, still seems to be missing from regional econometric models.

*Director, Economic Forecasting Project, Georgia State University.

Data deficiencies prevent any vigorous analysis of capital flows between regions or the full identification of trade patterns. Regional models have also ignored: the costs of overcoming distance; the related advantages of overcoming production thresholds through market expansion (e.g., import substitution and its causes); the intraregional reallocaton of resources to restore interregional factor price equalization when factor flows are more costly and less instantaneous than commodity flows; regional financial developments, or local disequilibrium conditions. Of course, many of these shortcomings are caused by data problems, especially by the absence of a rich menu of regional prices. However, other potential shortcomings, such as factor price equalization through intraregional resource reallocation, or the absence of regional financial markets, may not be problems at all. Where substantial data exists, such as with regional labor market information, underexploitation of regional economic theory has resulted in less than optimal use of the information at hand.

This paper is an attempt to outline a more general specification of the important labor market behavior that should be incorporated in regional econometric models. In analyzing labor markets, an income rather than an expenditures approach to regional modeling is utilized. However, only the labor market core of regional economies will be examined. Thus, nonlabor income, financial flows, regional prices, and tax receipts are not examined except in terms of their influence upon labor market behavior.

6.2 PRODUCTION RESPONSE

Because of data availability, regional analysis can be more fruitfully conducted by solving for all regional economic activity in terms of its labor market implications, than by concentrating upon commodity markets, such as with the Keynesian expenditures multiplier model. In particular, if the underlying production relationship has a constant elasticity of substitution, if firms maximize profits, and industries are in competitive equilibrium and experiencing a constant rate of technological improvement, the derived demand for labor inputs is:[6]

$$\log L_i = a^1 + b_1^1 t + b_2^1 \log(w/p) + b_3^1 \log Q_i \qquad (6.1)$$

where L_i = labor input in industry i, t is a time proxy to measure technological change, w/p is the hourly labor cost divided by the price of the product of industry i, and Q_i is the physical output of industry i. Also, $b_2 > 0$ and $b_1 > 0$ under normal conditions, while b_3 is the homogeneity factor and should be 1 under the above conditions.

The above relationship actually explains labor efficiency hours worked rather than people employed in industry. Because of costs associated with hiring and firing, and the presence of contractual arrangements, disparities between current employment and equilibrium employment can arise. A method for estimating the presence of these deviations from equilibrium relationships can be developed by exploiting the information on the workweek of production workers in manufacturing. This can be accomplished as follows: Assume equation (6.1) explains the derived demand for production worker hours. The non production workers (NP) in each industry are assumed to work a standard workweek. The derived demand for these labor services also may have a production relationship, where demand increases as normal production hours ($\bar{L}$) are expected to increase, and could appear as follows:

$$\log \text{NP}_i = a^2 + b_1^2 t + b_2^2 \log \frac{\text{WB}_i}{\text{WBP}_i} + b_3^2 \log \bar{L}_i \tag{6.2}$$

Unfortunately, the total wage bill (WB) is not known for each industry, although normal wage disbursements to production workers (WBP) are easily calculated by the hourly wage times normal workweek times annual weeks times production workers. Some adjustments will be needed, as outlined below, to convert production worker disbursements into production worker costs. The ratio of production to total wage costs can be calculated using the *Census of Manufacturers* and can then be extrapolated forward by assuming that changes in this ratio that occur nationally are also occurring regionally. (Some regional information is temporarily lost, but adjustments can be made when a new *Census* benchmark becomes available.) Depending upon the availability of data, several specifications of a lagged relationship could be used to estimate expected normal production hours from observations of actual hours worked.[7]

Because factor flows will be in terms of people, production hours need to be converted into workweeks and people. Costs are associated with hiring and terminating people, and are also borne by paying overtime premiums.[8] Assuming cost differences between changing people and changing hours for a given work complement remain relatively stable, hours will only temporarily differ from some normal workweek, e.g., as measured by a two year moving average of the workweek. Actual production worker workweeks will then depend upon the change in hours demanded and the deviation of the previous workweek from normal,

$$H_i = a^3 + b_1^3 (\Delta \log L_{it}) + b_2^3 \left(H_{it-1} \left(-\frac{1}{n} \sum_{j=1}^{n} H_{it-j} \right) \right) \tag{6.3}$$

where H_i = production worker workweek, $b_1 > 0$, $b_2 < 0$ to reflect the adjustment costs associated with changing hours versus people. Then

$$(L_i/H_i) + (NP_i) = E_i \qquad (6.4)$$

where E_i is employment in industry i.

Where data is not available, equations (6.2)–(6.4) could be omitted and E_i substituted for L_i in equation (6.1). (Indeed, this is necessary outside the manufacturing sector.) It should be clear, however, that substantial misspecification is introduced if the missing equations are appropriate.

6.2.1 Cyclical Changes in Labor Demand

Returning to equation (6.1), the estimated relationship is comparable to what Clower calls the notional demand for labor.[9] Of course, if no disequilibrium exists in regional labor markets, the notional and the effective demand for labor are identical. When economic activity declines cyclically, however, capital and labor probably both move down the prevailing production expansion path independently of any changes in labor costs or product prices that might establish a new optimum combination of labor and capital in equilibrium (i.e., production is quantity-oriented rather than price-responsive during contractions and their ensuing recoveries.) If $L_{it} < (1 - d)^t \bar{L}_i$, where $\bar{L}_i$ is the previous peak, d is the depreciation rate for capital, and $\bar{t}$ is the time since the previous peak, then

$$\text{Log } L_i = a + b_1' t + b_3 \text{Log } Q_i \qquad (6.1a)$$

where b_1' is only that portion of technological change that is totally independent of factor inputs. The rate of depreciation depends on the age distribution of the capital stock, which might be approximated by utilizing the secular growth rate of labor inputs (for example, an area with a 5 percent annual growth rate presumably has a newer average age of capital than a region with a 3 percent annual rate of growth). In other words, a movement along an expansion path, which is measured by the level of activity, rather than a shift in factor proportions, is relevant during periods of production disequilibrium.

Most regional models have been estimated in terms of equation (6.1a), which ignores the normal changes in factor demands that occur in an expanding area. However, the above discussion indicates that a stable labor demand relationship in terms of output does not exist. Rather, the demand for labor shifts, depending upon whether the industry is expanding or whether it is in contraction or recovery. In the latter instances, the response to aggregate demand alone is appropriate, but the relationship says little about relative regional development.

6.2.2 Converting Wage Disbursements into Wage Compensation

Returning to the notional demand for labor, several extensions are needed to provide a true regional demand equation. Labor costs usually are expressed as wage and salary disbursements rather than the more appropriate wage compensation. Ignoring differences in unemployment insurance schedules by state, the employer contributions for social insurance and other labor income (OLI) can be assigned to industries as follows:

$$\text{wage costs}_i = \text{wage disbursements}_i +$$

$$\frac{\text{wage disbursements}_i}{\text{U.S. wage disbursements}_i} \times (\text{U.S. OLI}_i)$$

$$+ \; \frac{(\text{U.S. Employer Soc. Sec.})}{(\text{U.S. Employee Soc. Sec.})} \times \text{employee S.S. contributions}_i \qquad (6.4)$$

To the extent that the annual national income by industry differentiates between shares of OLI or employer/employee social security contributions relative to wage disbursements, such information can be used to adjust shares of such employer labor costs. Particular regional cost factors, such as employer contributions at the state level for unemployment compensation; different annual wages by industry, which may change the effective payroll tax; or regional turnover rates, which influence insured unemployment payments, are also relevant and would need to be included. If they become elaborate enough and are important in determining regional competitiveness, a separate set of equations can be introduced assuming that independent estimates of wage costs can be derived:

$$\text{wage costs}_i - \text{wage disbursements}_i = a^4 + b_1^4 \, \text{Turnover}_i$$

$$+ \; b_2^4 \, \frac{\text{Annual Wage}_i}{\text{S.S. Wage Base}} + b_3^4 \, \text{U.S. OLI} + b_4^4 \, \frac{\text{U.S. employer S.S.}}{\text{U.S. employee S.S.}}$$

$$\times \; (\text{regional employee S.S.}) \times \frac{\text{Wage disbursements}_i}{\text{U.S. Wage disbursements}_i} \qquad (6.5)$$

If $b_4^4 = 1$, then it can be moved to the lefthand side of the equation. The *Census of Manufactures* may again provide periodic benchmarks for this discrepancy between wage costs and wage disbursements (assuming accruals can be ignored.)

6.2.3 Product Site Prices

Under ideal conditions, the product price contained in the substitution term in equation (6.1) should be the price received by the producer, excluding indirect taxes and transportation charges. However, these locationally important site prices generally are unavailable. Some local consumer price information is available, and it reveals that considerable differences in prices prevail throughout the country.

To partially compensate for this serious data limitation, the following procedure can be followed. Assume that all goods and services serving national markets have a national price; that is, use the relevant national procedure price by industry or industry deflator. All industries where production is less than local needs will respond to changes in national prices relative to local labor costs for their production decisions. For those firms producing beyond local needs, site costs must fall as transportation costs increase, if they are to remain competitive while national prices remain unchanged. Although cost discontinuties exist because of distance and because markets are not uniformly distributed, an increase in locational concentration can be assumed to reduce site receipts per unit for any given national price. Conversely, an increase in national prices with no increase in site costs will encourage increased locational concentration. It is reasonable to expect that as the firm services more than the local area, that is, as the relevant location quotient increases, a transportation cost adjustment to product price will rise exponentially. This occurs because the portion of total sales subject to transportation costs increases under these circumstances. Therefore, a possible specification becomes:

$$(\text{Location quotient})^{-a} \times \text{Product Price} \tag{6.6a}$$

leading to a new labor demand equation,

$$\text{Log } L_i = a^6 + b_1^6 t + b_2^6 \log \frac{(\text{labor cost})}{(\text{Product Price})}$$
$$+ b_3^6 \log \text{LQ}_i + b_4^6 \log Q_i \tag{6.6}$$

where LQ is the relevant location quotient and $b_3^6 = ab_2^6 < 0$.[10]

There are several problems with this specification. First, the location quotient should be included only when the site price differs from the market price. Given our assumptions, this occurs when the relevant location quotient exceeds 1. Otherwise, no adjustment may be needed for site prices. Second, the relevant location quotient may not use regional employment shares for its base. Industries that are market oriented may compare their employment concentration to the region's purchasing power concentration, $LQ_i = (L_i^R/L^{US}) / (RPI^R/RPI^{US})$. Industries which supply other industries should compare their concentration to those they serve within a region, $LQ_i = (L_i^R)/(L_j^R)_{j \neq i}$. For example, the chemicals industry in many southern states generally services the textile industry. A location quotient of 2 for textiles, indicating that textile employment's share of state employment is twice as great as it is nationally, almost certainly implies that some sales are in the national market, and therefore incurring transportation costs. A location quotient of 1.5 on the same basis for chemicals may not reflect a single ounce of product bearing substantial transportation costs, as all the product is going to the local textile companies.

Finally, the location quotient rises as labor inputs increase. The independent influence of market concentration upon the demand for labor may not be identifiable. A lagged location quotient would be less relevant, and would still create some statistical problems. If site prices were known, equations could be created for product prices in a similar manner to those for labor costs, and the "a" term for the location quotient could be determined in that specification. Alternately, different values for "a" can be assigned during the estimation of (6.6), permitting adjustments to the product price to be made directly.

It should be clear that location quotients serve as proxies for only one adjustment to product price, transportation costs. Differential indirect taxes, differential energy costs, or differential site prices for intermediate products, could all be used in the adjustment of product prices received by producers if information is known or proxies can be developed. For example, differential concentration ratios between industries and their primary suppliers may serve as proxies for transportation costs of materials. In this case, the location base is the concentration of suppliers, L_i^R/L_j^R, where j is the primary supplier to industry i in region R.

6.3 COMMODITY MARKET RESPONSE

Only the producers' production response to the quantities demanded for goods and services has been considered. The quantities demanded must now be determined. Many models estimate gross product originating by industry, and then use a host of regional or national variables to explain that measure. As data is not collected on gross product originating, many analysts use the Kendrick–Jaycox method to generate regional value added from the regional wage bill, by assuming the same factor shares exist regionally as nationally by industry.[11] While the assumption of constant factor shares may hold when the national demand for labor equals the effective demand for labor, the assumption breaks down when varying degrees of disequilibrium exist in regional labor markets. In essence, estimates of gross product originating remain appropriate using Kendrick–Jaycox techniques, either if w/p remains constant while $L_i < (1 - d)^t \bar{L}_i$, or if the labor market disequilibrium is similar nationally and regionally. This is unlikely, especially if prices are determined nationally while wage costs respond to local conditions.

Notwithstanding their estimation difficulties, two regional problems strongly suggest that estimates of gross product originating by industry are highly desirable. First, some price differentials may momentarily develop between the region and the nation, despite our general assumption that prices are determined nationally. (After all, that national price equation is altered by conditions in the regions.) This price competitiveness can best be estimated in terms of differential unit labor cost, which is developed with the aid of regional product originating estimates. Second, the quantity demanded differs locally from quantity supplied by changes in inventories to the extent that prices do not change to reflect local imbalances. While inventory measures are unavailable on a regional basis, implied inventory adjustments needed to restore momentary equilibrium in regional commodity markets, could be estimated using the behavior of labor market activity with the aid of an estimate of product originating.

When $L_i \geq (1 - d)^t \bar{L}_i$, the Kendrick–Jaycox estimates are perfectly adequate approximations. Otherwise, both the utilization of capital and labor are reduced by the labor market inequality. Assume that the wage bill for industry i in a region is $250 million and that national factor shares lead to an estimate for other value added of $100 million. Then L_i falls 5 percent. Other value added would fall to $95 million even if the wage bill expanded as a result of local increases in the wage rate. As long as disequilibrium persists, it is presumed that production moves along the same activity path independent of price fluctuations. When equilibrium is reestablished, the return to Kendrick–Jaycox estimates may require significant changes (for some firms in the region were probably expanding and responding to equilibrium conditions throughout the disequilibrium period). After a new peak has been reached, any discrepancy between the new national standard and the disequilibrium estimate could be allocated across the disequilibrium period to eliminate the discrepancy. These estimates of gross product originating will differ from the Kendrick-Jaycox estimates as a result of differences between the regional and national magnitude of labor market disequilibrium.

Deflators for product originating by industry in the nation can be used to derive industrial output, adjusted for price changes, only if the discrepancy between sales and value added remains unchanged between the region and the nation. Of course, such assumptions are not valid, as the discussion concerning site price clearly indicates. Purchased services, such as transportation costs, may be rising or declining in the region. The production specification is already designed to respond to such differentials. Also, the price index still may be valid locally as well as nationally, if prices of purchased services are changing similarly in both areas. Thus, such an assumption poses no serious problems, except in times of rapidly rising energy or materials prices, where usage per unit of output differs by region.

Real gross product originating by sector measures the producer response to economic conditions. This quantity supplied differs from the quantity demanded by the change in inventories. Therefore, an explanation of real gross product originating requires both an explanation of the quantity demanded from a region's industry, and an explanation of why production differs from that demand (an increase in desired inventories to meet increased transactions should be incorporated in the demand relationship). Because there are costs to altering production, this period's quantity supplied will be the same as in the last period unless (1) expected sales have changed, (2) last period's production was inappropriate (or will be inappropriate if continued because it was eliminating some disequilibrium), or (3) the expected cost of holding inventories has changed.

Expected sales can be either for final users locally and nationally or as inputs into other producers' processes. In the latter case, major input-output relationships could be used to explain the interindustry portion of quantity demanded. However, an increase in the activity to which a regional firm is a basic supplier would already be reflected in the site cost adjustments that express the competitiveness of regional plants, as discussed earlier, if the location quotients are appropriately constructed. Thus, further adjustments should not be required. Indeed, local expansion of the textile industry may not create increased local demand for chemicals if the site costs have increased as a result of forces within the chemicals industry. On the other hand, increased textile activity nationally could stimulate local chemical sales even if the local textile industry does not share in this expansion, especially if national capacity for dyes and related chemicals becomes fully utilized. This would argue for a national output originating measure for the industry(ies) that other industries naturally supply, in addition to any measures of basic national expenditures variables.

6.3.1 Regional Competitiveness

Thus far, prices were assumed to depend on national markets, while profit-ability, and therefore the local decision to produce, depended on site costs and site revenues. However, regions increase or lose their markets by changing prices in relation to competitors. One instrument that can be used to measure regional competitiveness by industry is relative unit labor costs. (Total factor costs are more appropriate but are generally difficult to measure.) If national deflators are used to measure the volume of product originating by industry, unit labor costs then can be measured by dividing the wage-cost measure by the price-adjusted product measure.[12] (If the disequilibrium procedure is used to construct the estimate of products originating, deviations from capacity production will be captured in this measure.)

Finally, the product originating in an industry may depend upon the local demand for that activity. As the local market expands, more units of activity can be sold at site prices that approach national revenues per unit, in other words, transportation charges are minimal. These conditions could be captured in a location quotient product price adjustment, and will be for those industries that have high location quotients. For those industries without such adjustments (because they are totally responsive to local conditions), the problem is one of meeting local needs, subject to import substitution or reduced competitiveness with other regions.

The above argument leads to the following specification for expected real output originating by industry:

$$Q_i^e = a^{7'} + b_1^{7'} \frac{ULC_i^R}{ULC_i^{US}} + b_2^{7'} Q_i^{US} + b_3^{7'} Q^{US}$$

$$+ b_4^{7'} (Q^R \text{ or } RPI^R). \tag{6.7a}$$

where Q_i^e is expected output originating in industry i, ULC_i^R is unit labor costs in industry i in the region, ULC_i^{US} is unit labor costs in industry i in the nation, Q_i^{US} is output originating in industry i in the nation, and Q^{US} and Q^R or RPI^R are national and regional measures of aggregate real output or purchasing power.

Collinearity problems are probably extensive in the above specification. If a multiplicative relationship is a reasonable approximation (it is a demand relationship), then shares can be used in the estimation procedure:

$$\log Q_i^e = a^7 + b_1^7 \log \frac{ULC_i^R}{ULC_i^{US}} + b_2^7 \log \frac{(Q_i^{US})}{(Q^{US})} +$$

$$b_3^7 \log Q^{US} + b_4^7 (Q^R/Q^{US}) \text{ (or } RPI^R/RPI^{US}) \tag{6.7}$$

where

$$b_3^7 = b_3^{7'} - b_2^{7'} - b_4^{7'} \text{ if } b_2^{7'} = b_2^7 \text{ and } b_4^{7'} = b_4^7.$$

When regional forces dominate, the regional variable and the regional share are substituted for the national variable and the regional share.

Two other arguments are used to estimate the actual output originating by industry. First, goods-producing industries may change their desire to hold inventories relative to sales because of changes in the expected costs of holding inventories, such as storage and finance costs less expected capital gains. Second, the commodities market may be out-of-equilibrium in relation to expected sales. This commodities market disequilibrium is manifested by undesired inventory levels for goods producers, or undesired capacity utilization, for the nongoods sectors.

If storage costs can be ignored, the shift in desired inventories depends upon finance costs less expected gains. While many models ignore financial variables, or incorporate them in their measures of national output originating, it appears that distance from investors may influence the financial rating received by an industry for any given risk that its activities may imply. Market information is not costless. It therefore seems likely that a capital deficit region will have a higher marginal product of capital in equilibrium than would a capital surplus region.[13] Furthermore, increased intraregional generation of funds will tend to reduce the discrepancy. (Government restrictions also may cause less than complete equality of earnings by investors between regions.) No flow-of-funds accounts are yet possible by region, but commercial and industrial loans (CI) at commercial banks could serve as a proxy for regional borrowing capacity for industries, while savings and loan activity (changes in mortgages outstanding) could dictate the financing of single-family homes. Thus, short-term interest rates could be adjusted for the local concentration of commercial and industrial loans, $(CI^R/PQ^R / CI^{US}/PQ^{US})^a \times r$, where PQ is the current value of output and r is the relevant interest rate. Construction product originating may use housing as an argument, where activity is explained partially for single-family units with the use of mortgage activity at the regional savings and loan associations. Expected price changes could then be estimated by using a lagged relationship on recent prices.[14]

Whether consideration of shifts in the desired holdings of inventories will be important at the regional level must await empirical investigation. The adjustment to disequilibrium in the commodities market is another matter. Differential regional cycles may be caused by this problem (at least in construction, if not in other sectors as well), and these cycles could influence factor flows, leading to significantly different growth rates for seemingly similar regional economies.

Inventory data is not sufficiently available at the regional level to be used to measure commodity market disequilibrium. Therefore, some instruments must be created that are closely related to the underlying disequilibrium behavior. As changes in production are costly, any significant changes from normal rates of expansion probably represent either a substantial shift in equilibrium conditions or a reaction to accumulating imbalances. While the speed of adjustment to disequilibrium may vary, many inventory imbalances are eliminated within five quarters.[15] If last period's growth in output was significantly different from growth rates for the previous five quarters, it is probable that imbalances had become so substantial that a production adjustment was desired. As adjustments are almost never completed within the quarter that they are started, such deviation from previous growth rates will probably persist in the current quarter.

Let GQ designate a one period growth rate for Q. Then

$$(\partial Q_{i_{t-1}}/\partial t) - (GQ_{i_{t-1}} - \tfrac{1}{5} \sum_{j=2}^{6} GQ_{i_{t-j}}) > 0.$$

Using the expected output of (6.7), remembering that production decisions are costly, and designating any changes in logarithmic relationships between two periods as G, one can use the following specification for real product originating by industry:

$$GQ_i = a^{8'} + b_1^{8'} G\left(\frac{ULC_i^R}{ULC_i^{US}}\right) + b_2^{8'} G(Q_i^{US}/Q^{US})$$

$$+ b_3^{8'} GQ^{US} + b_4^{8'} G(Q^R/Q^{US})$$

$$+ b_5^{8'} G\left(\frac{CI^R}{PQ^R} \Big/ \frac{CI^{US}}{PQ^{US}}\right) + b_6^{8'} G(r - pe)$$

$$b_7^{8'}(GQ_{it-1} - \tfrac{1}{5} \sum_{j=2}^{6} GQ_{it-j}) ,^{16} \tag{6.8a}$$

where all the variables have previously been defined except $(r - pe)$, which is some measure of the real interest rate. Of course, these important disequilibrium problems require quarterly information. Furthermore, b_2, b_3, b_5, and b_6 may be irrelevant in specifications where inventory accumulations are not significant, or where local variables are dominant. Also, b_7 may be altered depending on what disequilibrium measure is appropriate in the commodities market. Because of the inherent noise in data available at the regional level, the use of quarterly growth rates could create significant measurement difficulties. In that case, a less precise but more workable specification would be $Q_{it} = S_i^e +$ disequilibrium response.

If expected sales (S^e) follow the adaptive pattern with a Koyck transformation, the specification for (6.8a) becomes:

$$\log Q_i = a^8 + b_1^8 \log \frac{(\text{ULC}_i^R)}{(\text{ULC}_i^{US})} +$$

$$+ b_2^8 \log (Q_i^{US}/Q^{US}) + b_3^8 \log Q^{US} \qquad (6.8)$$

$$+ b_4^8 \log (Q^R/Q^{US}) + b_5^8 \log \frac{\text{CI}^R}{\text{PQ}^R} \Big/ \frac{\text{CI}^{US}}{\text{PQ}^{US}}$$

$$+ b_6^8 \, \Theta_i^n \, (r_{t-i} - P_{t-i}) + b_8^8 \log Q_{it-1}$$

$$+ b_7^8 \, (GQ_{it-1} - \tfrac{1}{5} \sum_{j=2}^{6} GQ_{it-j})$$

where Θ_i^n is a lagged operator. The danger here is that the lagged dependent variable would capture more explanatory power than is justified, especially as the disequilibrium response may be incorrect and measurement errors may be significant in many of the other variables.

6.3.2 Construction Sector

The commodities market disequilibrium that is described in (6.8) may need to be so mechanistic only for the manufacturing and mining sectors. In construction, equilibrium conditions are related to growth in the local economy. Regardless of the location quotient, the products of construction are not exported (excluding a bridge or a dam, which may influence two regions.) Construction is not a single product. Disaggregation into residential, private nonresidential, and identifiable public categories would be desirable. Disequilibrium and the response to such commodity imbalances also should be considered by category. Unfortunately, most employment information cannot be matched to the separate construction sectors. While any disaggregation that is desirable can be used in the explanation of output originating in construction, one employment relationship still may be the greatest employment detail possible.

Assume construction is a single homogeneous commodity. As an investment good, construction is valued for the output of goods and services that it creates. If desired construction stock is K^*, then $K^* = f(Q^e)$. Output originating in construction (Q_c) is replacing worn-out construction goods, meeting changes in K^*, or altering previous imbalances: $Q_c = \Delta K^* + \delta(K - K^*) + dK$ where d is the rate of replacement of existing capital.

In equilibrium, $Q_c^* = a\Delta\bar{Q} + ad\bar{Q}$ or $Q_c^*/\bar{Q} = a\Delta\bar{Q}/\bar{Q} + ad$, where $\bar{Q}$ is equilibrium output. Clearly, the share of construction in total regional activity depends upon the rate of growth of the region and the rate of replacement of existing capital. If the same magnitude of imbalance existed at the two most recent cyclical peaks for construction's share of actual regional output, and if some average depreciation rate can be assigned for that period, a desired share of construction activity in terms of current growth rates can be estimated. The magnitude of imbalance then can be measured by comparing the actual activity to the desired activity over the relevant period,

$$\sum_{i=1}^{n} \{Q_{c_{t-i}} - (Q_c^*/Q)_{t-i} \times Q_{t-i}\},$$

where $(Q_c^*/Q)_{t-1} = aG_{Q_{t-1}} + ad$ and a is a parameter that is explained above. Q_c^e may be more highly related to population (or adult population) than to regional output, as it is the output that is expected at the completion of construction activity. Also, the response to imbalances and the rate of depreciation may both be constrained by financial variables; that is, $(MO^R/PQ^R) / (MO^{US}/PQ^{US})$ times imbalances might be used to express these constraints, where MO is mortgages outstanding. This leads to the following construction equation:

$$Q_c = b_1^9 \underset{i}{\Theta} \text{Pop}_i + b_2^9 \sum_{i=1}^{n} \{Qc_{t-i} - (Q\overset{*}{c}/Q)_{t-i} \times Q_{t-i}\} + b_3^9 t$$

$$+ b_4^9 \frac{MO^R}{PQ^R} / \frac{MO^{US}}{PQ^{US}} + b_5^9 \{Qc_{t-1} - (Q\overset{*}{c}/Q)_{t-1} \times Q_{t-1})\} + a^9 \tag{6.9}$$

where ΘPop_i reflects a lagged relationship in terms of the relevant population.

6.3.3 Transportation, Communication, and Utilities

The transportation, communication, and utility (TCU) group either distributes services to the goods producing sector or transports the output of that sector. While some residents also receive services, this industry responds more closely with goods activity. It keeps no inventory of goods, but undoubtedly maintains a buffer capacity. (The notional demand for labor is not disturbed when this buffer changes, although such changes will alter the response of this sector to demand conditions.) This buffer probably is excessive if the share of TCU to goods activity is growing sharply. A reasonable specification is as follows:

$$\log Q_{\text{TCU}} = a^{10} + b_1^{10} \log\left(\frac{\text{ULC}_{\text{TCU}}^{\text{R}}}{\text{ULC}_{\text{TCU}}^{\text{US}}}\right) + b_2^{10} \log\left(Q_G^{\text{US}}/Q_G^{\text{R}}\right) + b_3^{10} \log Q_G^{\text{R}}$$

$$+ b_4^{10} \log Q_{\text{TCU}_{t-1}} + b_5^{10} \left\{\left(\frac{Q_{\text{TCU}}}{Q_G}\right)_{t-1} - \frac{1}{n} \sum_{i=1}^{n} \left(\frac{Q_{\text{TCU}}}{Q_G}\right)_{t-i}\right\} \times Q_G \quad (6.10)$$

where Q_G is output originating in the relevant goods producing industry.

6.3.4 Wholesale Trade

Wholesale trade is similar to TCU, except that it also responds to retail activity and rises when imbalances are growing in goods production because of the need to handle involuntary inventories.

$$\log Q_{\text{WT}} = a^{11} + b_1^{11} \log \frac{(\text{ULC}_{\text{WT}}^{\text{R}})}{(\text{ULC}_{\text{WT}}^{\text{US}})} + \left(b_2^{11} \log Q_G^{\text{US}}/Q_G^{\text{R}}\right)$$

$$+ b_3^{11} (Q_G^{\text{R}} + Q_{\text{RT}}^{\text{R}}) + b_4^{11} \log Q_{\text{WT}_{t-1}} + b_5^{11} \left\{\left(\frac{Q_{\text{WT}}}{Q_G}\right)_{t-1} - \frac{1}{5} \sum_{i=1}^{5} \left(\frac{Q_{\text{WT}}}{Q_G}\right)_{t-i}\right\}$$

$$\times Q_G + b_6^{11} (Q_{\text{RT}} - Q_{\text{RT}_{t-1}}) + b_7^{11} \left(\frac{\text{CI}^{\text{R}}}{\text{PQ}^{\text{R}}} \Big/ \frac{\text{CI}^{\text{US}}}{\text{PQ}^{\text{US}}}\right) \quad (6.11)$$

where RT denotes activity in retail trade.

6.3.5 Retail Trade, Finance, Private Services

Retail trade, finance, and private services are all related to local purchasing power, although they may also rise or fall as a result of net tourist expenditures (local purchases of nonresidents minus foreign purchases by residents.) some models have assumed that only local conditions affect these sectors. However, import substitution or the extension of the service areas of cities can increase this activity in addition to the influence of increased regional purchasing power. Also, buffer capacity exists in these sectors as well.

$$
\log Q_{RT} = a^{12} + b^{12}_1 \log \frac{ULC^R_{RT}}{ULC^{US}_{RT}} + b^{12}_2 \log\left(RPI^{US}/RPI^R\right) + b^{12}_3 \overset{m}{\underset{i}{\theta}} \log RPI^R
$$

$$
+ b^{12}_4 \left\{ \left(\frac{Q_{RT}}{RPI}\right)_{t-1} - \frac{1}{n} \sum_{i=1}^{n} \left(\frac{Q_{RT}}{RPI}\right)_{t-i} \right\} \times RPI + b^{12}_5 \left(\frac{IL^R}{PQ^R} \middle/ \frac{IL^{US}}{PQ^{US}}\right)
$$

$$
+ b^{12}_6 \left\{ \left(\frac{Q_{RT}}{RPI}\right)_{t-1} - \left(\frac{Q_{RT}}{RPI}\right)_{t-2} \right\} \tag{6.12}
$$

where

$$
\frac{IL^R}{PQ^R} \middle/ \frac{IL^{US}}{PQ^{US}}
$$

is the concentration of installment loans in the area and RPI is a measure of real purchasing power.

$$
\log Q_{SER} = a^{13} + b^{13}_1 \log \frac{ULC^R_{SER}}{ULC^{US}_{SER}} + b^{13}_2 \log (RPI^{US}/RPI^R)
$$

$$
+ b^{13}_3 \overset{m}{\underset{i}{\theta}} \log RPI^R_{t-i} + b^{13}_4 \left\{ \left(\frac{Q_{SER}}{RPI}\right)_{t-1} - \frac{1}{n} \sum_{i=1}^{n} \left(\frac{Q_{SER}}{RPI}\right)_{t-i} \right\} \times RPI
$$

$$
+ b^{13}_5 \left\{ \left(\frac{Q_{SER}}{RPI}\right)_{t-1} - \left(\frac{Q_{SER}}{RPI}\right)_{t-2} \right\} \tag{6.13}
$$

$$
\log Q_{FIR} = a^{14} + b^{14}_1 \log \frac{ULC^R_{FIR}}{ULC^{US}_{FIR}} + b^{14}_2 \log (RPI^{US}/RPI^R)
$$

$$
+ b^{14}_3 \overset{m}{\underset{i}{\theta}} \log RPI^R_{t-i} + b^{14}_4 \log Qc + b^{14}_5 \left\{ \left(\frac{Q_{FIR}}{RPI}\right)_{t-1} - \frac{1}{n} \sum_{i=1}^{n} \left(\frac{Q_{FIR}}{RPI}\right)_{t-i} \right\}
$$

$$
\times RPI + b^{14}_6 \left\{ \left(\frac{Q_{FIR}}{RPI}\right)_{t-1} - \left(\frac{Q_{FIR}}{RPI}\right)_{t-2} \right\} + b^{14}_7 \log (CI/P). \tag{6.14}
$$

The addition of Qc is to reflect the importance of construction for real estate brokers, while CI/P is the deflated value of a major portion of regional bank loans and is used to reflect bank activity. (Regional financial variables must at least influence employment in financial institutions.)

6.3.6 Agriculture & Government

Only agriculture and government remain to be considered. A production relationship is increasingly valid for agriculture, but output originating depends on values of crops and the efficiency of the land, which varies with the weather. The increased complexity that would be required to describe the agricultural economy is not justified for most states. For this reason, output originating in agriculture (but not the employment derived from it) will probably remain exogenous in the shortrun and be related to regional shares of the national market for longer-term projections.

Although some cost minimization production relationship probably exists for the production of government goods and services, output originating in the government sector does not appropriately measure public output. Furthermore, location of some federal government activities, especially the military, may not depend on direct cost minimization factors. Nevertheless, these local concentrations of federal activity are not totally exogenous.

For example, changes in the share of domestically domiciled military personnel residing in a region may depend upon the change in domestically domiciled personnel (training bases will accentuate any fluctuation), and probably upon the economic importance or the aerospace importance of the region:

$$\text{Mil}^R/\text{Mil}^{US} = a^{15} + b^{15}_1 \text{GMil}^{US} + b^{15}_2 Q^R/Q^{US}$$

$$(\text{or, } b^{15}_{2,} \text{LQ}_{\text{AERO}} + b^{15}_3 (\text{Mil}^R/\text{Mil}^{US})_{t-1}) \tag{6.15}$$

where Mil is the number of military personnel and LQ_{AERO} is the location quotient of the aerospace industry.

Federal civilian employees might be treated similarly, with the exception that many of their programs may be more people- or household-oriented than income-oriented, and might not have as obvious a permanent to training dichotomy as the military. Also, distances appear to affect federal concentration decisions, such that heavy concentrations appear to be dissipated over time. Because of national wage standards and standardized production conditions, other cost minimization forces do not appear to be present. Therefore,

$$\text{FED}^R/\text{FED}^{US} = a^{16} + b^{16}_1(\text{Pop}^R/\text{Pop}^{US}) + b^{16}_2\left(\frac{\text{FED}^R}{\text{Pop}^R} \Big/ \frac{\text{FED}^{US}}{\text{Pop}^{US}}\right)_{t-1}$$

$$+ b^{16}_3 \frac{\text{MIL}^R}{\text{MIL}^{US}} + b^{16}_4\left(\frac{\text{FED}^R}{\text{FED}^{US}}\right)_{t-1} \tag{6.16}$$

where $b^{16}_2 < 0$.

State and local government expenditures are dependent upon regional economic conditions and/or intergovernmental grants. Most governments are constitutionally constrained from borrowing to finance operating expenses, and therefore must finance government services from an expanded tax base, changes in tax rates, or temporary restraints on wages paid to personnel. A control problem could be established, using tax rate changes, deviations from competitive wages, employment, and purchases, as decision variables subject to the constraints that no borrowing for operating budgets is permitted; however, the difficulty of measuring government's objective function still exists.

Several models have used government employment as a proxy for government output. This assumes that public output is proportional to real expenditures, value added is proportional to purchases, and employment is proportional to value added. In the absence of further information, an assumption that a *normal* wage bill is proportional to public output may be unavoidable, but the employment component of that wage bill can easily be altered by restraining wages in an effort to purchase more personnel.

Conceptually, the observed value added by state and local government (which is the wage bill plus supplements for state and local employees) may be the result of adjusting to a desired value added by altering wages (employment is needed to meet desired services) or taxes relative to normal desired levels:

$$VA = b_1 VA^* + B_2 (\overline{WBill} - WBill)$$
$$+ b_3 \left(\frac{\overline{TREV}}{PQ^R} - \frac{TREV}{PQ^R} \right) \times PQ^R + b_4 VA_{t-1} + a \qquad (6.17a)$$

where $b_2, b_3 < 0$, VA is value added in state and local government, WBill is the wage bill, TREV is total revenues, the bars represent equilibrium values, and the asterisk is the desired value added. Desired real value added may change with changes in population, population requiring education, normal real output, and the resources extracted from nongovernmental use:

$$VA^*/P_G = a + b_1 Pop + b_2 (Pop^{65-16}/Pop)$$
$$+ b_3 Q^{R^*} + b_4 \frac{TREV}{(PQ^R - VA)} \qquad (6.17b)$$

In this context, the price of a unit of government is the labor cost per unit of government employment. However, such costs can be restrained temporarily for budgetary reasons. Thus, P_G should be a price index based on competitive, rather than actual, governmental wages.

Competitive wages would result from the demand and the supply conditions for government employment if the government did not temporarily exert its monopsony powers to meet desired services. Actual government wages differ from competitive wages as a result of imbalances between the quantity demanded and the funding of government services. Of course, equation (6.17b) can be solved for the ratio of desired real value added to real regional product. As real value added is equivalent to government employment, the equilibrium relationship becomes a ratio of desired employment to real regional product $(\mathrm{EMP}_G / Q^R)^*$. The measure of imbalance then becomes

$$\left(\frac{\mathrm{EMP}_G}{Q^R}\right) - \left(\frac{\mathrm{EMP}_G}{Q^R}\right)^*.$$

While the desired ratio remains unknown, some prior constraints and an iterative estimation procedure can be used to approximate its value. If revenues fall short of meeting desired levels because Q^R falls short of expectations, desired value added will be achieved by restraining wages. The actual employment-output ratio would exceed the desired condition. The reverse is unlikely, for it would require paying more than competitive wages while restraining employment growth. Therefore, the employment-output ratio either exceeds desired conditions or is equivalent to it.

If the imbalance is independent of the right-hand variables in equation (6.17b), the actual ratio can be used to generate approximate estimates of the parameters in that relationship. The resulting misspecifications (equation (6.17b) explains desired, not actual, ratios) will bias the estimated parameters. However, if the ratio derived from these estimated parameters is to serve as an instrument for the desired ratio, it cannot exceed the actual ratio. As long as no parameter is more biased than any other, those observations in which the ratios estimated from the parameters and right-hand variables exceed the actual ratios are most likely to correspond to conditions where imbalances are small (or nonexistent). Thus, specification error will be reduced if the parameters are re-estimated with only these observations. The resulting parameters, when used to generate a predicted ratio for the entire set of observations, should greatly reduce the number of negative imbalances. If enough observations remain to provide meaningful estimates of the parameters, the procedure could be repeated. Once the estimation is concluded, all the parameters can be reduced by whatever scalar is needed to insure that estimated values will never be greater than actual values.

This derived measure of imbalance can be used in the government wage equation in which,

$$\text{Wages}_G = f\left\{X, \left(\frac{\text{EMP}_G}{Q^R} - \frac{\widehat{\text{EMP}_G}}{Q^R}\right)\right\} \tag{6.17c}$$

where $\partial \text{ wages}_G / \partial \text{imbalance} < 0$, X are any other relevant variables, and $\widehat{\text{EMP}_G} / Q^R$ is the employment ratio derived from equation (6.17b), after the latter is estimated by the iterative technique described above.[17] Then competitive wages are derived from equation (6.17c) by assuming the imbalances are zero. This measure of competitive wages can be used to create P_G in equation (6.17b). In addition, the competitive wage multiplied by current employment can be used for $\overline{\text{WBill}}$.

The remaining unknown in equation (6.17a), $\overline{\text{TREV}}$, can be measured as that TREV in equation (6.17b), which will eliminate any imbalances in the wage equation.[17] This leads to the following equation for state and local government value-added:

$$VA = a^{17} + b_1^{17} PG + b_2^{17} PG \times \text{Pop} + b_3^{17} PG \times \frac{\text{Pop}^{65-16}}{\text{Pop}} + b_4^{17} PG$$

$$\times Q^{R*} + b_5^{17} PG \times \frac{\text{TREV}}{(PQ^R - VA)} + b_6^{17} (\overline{\text{WBill}} - \text{WBill}) + b_7^{17} (\overline{\text{TREV}}$$

$$- \text{TREV}) + b_8^{17} VA_{t-1} \tag{6.17}$$

Once a specification for equation (6.17c) is made, employment is calculated as:

$$\text{EMP}_{S\&L} = \frac{VA\text{-}SUP}{\text{Wage}_{S\&L}} \tag{6.18}$$

where SUP is the supplementary wage income of state and local employees and is either exogenous or a ratio of VA.

6.4 LABOR RESPONSE

Ideally, each sector would have a labor supply relationship to correspond to its derived demand for labor. A disequilibrium term would then be used to measure the unemployment prevailing in each sector at a given wage.[18] However, labor skills are more uniform than the goods and services represented by the production relationships, although they are not sufficiently homogeneous to be considered a single labor pool from which skills are allocated to the separate sectors. Because of an absence of data on occupational skills, it is useful to consider each sector as if it has a separate supply relationship. (The composition of skills required are assumed to be changing slowly. Thus, equilibrium wage differentials reflect differences in the skills composition.) However, the supply of labor services in the region will be allocated to each sector in accordance with its differential wage. This procedure also permits a reallocation of resources within the region, to satisfy the factor price equalization principle when interregional trade encounters some friction. The supply price of labor inputs in each sector should rise with employment in that sector, commodity prices, taxes per unit of labor for the region (sector information would be more desirable but is unavailable), other regional wages, and nonlabor purchasing power. This latter term should include the asset holdings of households, as well as all nonlabor income for those potentially offering labor services, but such data is not available.[19] In addition, some wages are negotiated at the national rather than regional level. Thus, a portion of each sector's wages will not respond in the shortrun to local conditions. In some sectors, the minimum wage or other regulated labor market characteristics may also be relevant.

Such a relationship holds only when labor markets are in equilibrium. As disequilibrium is possible in production relationships, it also is possible in supply conditions, especially when $L_i < (1 - d_L)^f \bar{L}_i$. (Just as capital was constructed to provide tools for peak labor, skills may have been developed for that one industry — industry-specific training. Similarly, the degree of disequilibrium will diminish over time as such labor becomes absorbed in alternative occupations or emigrates from the area.) The degree of dispersal of any disequilibrium must depend upon general labor market conditions in the region. This problem can be partially resolved with the aid of the following geometric adjustment mechanism:

$$\log W_{i_t} - \log W_{i_{t-4}} = \gamma \log W^*_{i_t} - \gamma \log W_{i_{t-4}} + e_t {}^{[20]} \qquad (6.19a)$$

where $\gamma = a$ UNEM (unemployment rate), W^*_i is the desired wage for industry i, and W is the actual wage. Thus, any desired wage will be adjusted slowly, with the speed of adjustment depending on the proportion unemployed. Ideally, UNEM should be the deviation from some natural rate of unemployment, but the above specification is adequate as long as the natural rate has not changed significantly within a region.

Even with the above adjustment, a labor supply specification that permits intraregional factor flows and responsiveness to national wage settlements suffers from colinearity problems. If comparisons with other regional wages can be used in place of the level of regional and national wages, the desired wage equation becomes:

$$W_i^* = a + b_1\,\text{EMP}_i + b_2\,(W_i/W^R)_{t-1}$$

$$+\ b_3\,(W_i^{US}/W^R) + b_4\,\text{CPI}_{t-1}$$

$$+\ b_5\,\frac{\text{NLI}^R}{\text{CPI}}_{t-1}/\text{EMP}^R + b_6\,\frac{\text{WTAX}}{\text{WB}} + b_7\,\text{WMIN} \qquad (6.19\text{b})$$

where NLI^R is nonlabor income in the region, CPI is the consumer price index, WTAX is the payroll tax paid by employees, WMIN is a variable that reflects the minimum wage, and W is the wage rate in industry i, or for the entire region or nation if no subscript is present.

This does not address the problem of prevailing labor supply disequilibrium within a sector. One alternative is to assume that $b_1 = 0$ when $L_i < (1 - d_L)^t\,\bar{L}_i$, but this does not permit downward adjustments when disequilibrium is substantial. Thus, the addition of a disequilibrium term is preferred. Moreover, d_L, the rate of decay in human capital designed for industry i, is an unknown, and certainly must depend upon the region's prevailing unemployment. This area must be studied further. In the meantime, values between .005 and .02 can be assigned to d_L on a quarterly basis, with the preferred rate dependent on the explained variation of the dependent variable and the signs of b_1 and b_8 in the following equation. With these adjustments, the labor supply equation becomes:

$$\log W_{it} - \log W_{it-4} = a^{19} + b_1^{19}\,\text{UNEM}\,\log\overset{\Lambda}{\text{EMP}}_i + b_2^{19}\,\text{UNEM}\,\log$$

$$(W_i/W^R)_{t-1} + b_3^{19}\,\text{UNEM}\,\log\,(W_i^{US}/W^R) + b_4^{19}\,\text{UNEM}\,\log\,\text{CPI}_{t-1}^R$$

$$+\ b_5^{19}\,\text{UNEM}\,\log\,\{(\text{NLI}^R/\text{CPI})\,/\,\text{EMP}^R\} + b_6^{19}\,\text{UNEM}\,\log\,\frac{\text{WTAX}}{\text{WB}}$$

$$+\ b_7^{19}\,\text{UNEM}\,\log\,\text{WMIN} + b_8^{19}\,\text{UNEM}\,\log\,\{(1-d_L)^t(\overline{\text{EMP}}_i - \text{EMP}_i)\}$$

$$+\ b_9^{19}\,\log W_{it-4} \qquad (6.19)$$

where $b_1, b_3, b_4, b_5, b_6, b_7 > 0$, and b_2, b_8, and $b_9 < 0$, $\overset{\Lambda}{\text{EMP}}$ is an estimate of EMP to adjust for simultaneous equation bias, and $\overline{\text{EMP}}_i$ is previous peak employment. Not all the variables may always be relevant, and b_8 should only be included when the value in parentheses is positive. Also, the production and labor supply conditions are simultaneous relationships requiring appropriate instruments to identify the parameters.

The production and wage equations establish the equality between effective demand and effective supply. However, substantial disequilibrium can exist under those conditions. In order to measure the number unemployed, which partially reflects this disequilibrium, labor force participation rates can be estimated. The population 16 + is known only annually, but the implied migration can be allocated among the quarters. Once this quarterly series is constructed, changes in participation rates can be related to real wages, nonlabor income per capita, taxes, commodity prices, and employment opportunities, very much as in the sector supply equations, e.g.:

$$\log \frac{LF}{Pop16+} = a^{20} + b^{20}_1 \log \frac{W^R}{CPI^R} /(Pop\ 16+)_{t-1} + b^{20}_3 \log \frac{WTAX}{WB}$$

$$+ b^{20}_4 \log CPI_{t-1} + b^{20}_5 (\log EMP_t - \log EMP_{t-1}) \tag{6.20}$$

Finally, any imbalance between regions in employment opportunities or real earnings will cause labor to migrate. Presumably, distance also matters in the migration decision. Significant differences in earnings or employment opportunities will have a greater impact if they are near. At this time, the region will be compared only to the remainder of the United States.

Again, some device may be needed to allocate the annual migration figures to quarterly patterns. While many studies show that in-migration and out-migration may be based upon different economic forces, using a formulation for the net change may not create substantial problems. Other studies have also indicated that civilian migration responds to military flows, as families follow their household head. (This is a measurement problem rather than a behavioral problem, but should be included in any analysis.) Also, the natural unemployment rate may be different in different regions because of underlying demographic characteristics or differences in work-leisure alternatives. Thus, differences in the unemployment rate between regions do not measure differences in employment opportunities. However, the following specification may provide an explanation of population flows:

$$MIG = a^{21} + b^{21}_1 \overset{n}{\underset{i}{\theta}} \left(\frac{W^R/CPI^R}{W^{US}/CPI^{US}}\right)_{-i} + b^{21}_2 \overset{m}{\underset{j}{\theta}} (\Delta EMP - \Delta LF^N)_{-j}$$

$$+ b^{21}_3 \left(UNEM_{t-1} - \frac{1}{n} \overset{n}{\underset{i-1}{\Sigma}} UNEM_{-i}\right) + b^{21}_4 \Delta MIL$$

$$+ b^{21}_5 \times \left(\frac{WTAX^R}{WB^R} / \frac{WTAX^{US}}{WB^{US}}\right) \tag{6.21}$$

where ΔLF^N is derived by multiplying the current participation rate by the natural change in population 16+, and W^R and W^{US} are average annual wage earnings per worker.

6.5 CONCLUSION

The above model is not complete, for it excludes such important variables as regional prices, nonlabor income, tax receipts, and financial flows. In addition, several equations are needed to advance from the sector wage bills to wage disbursements in the personal income accounts. All these issues are important in closing the systems, and some, such as the property earnings of households or implicit financing needs of regional enterprises, may contain important regional factors. However, this attempt to develop a more generalized regional statement of labor market conditions, the core of regional models, has already required a substantial amount of new development.

Disequilibrium conditions have been introduced into the demand and supply for labor. Distances have been implicitly introduced with the aid of location quotients. A procedure for analyzing interregional discrepancies between labor costs and wage disbursements has been identified. Possible measurement errors when commodity markets are in disequilibrium have been identified when the Kendrick–Jaycox procedure is used to measure regional output originating. Special inventory problems for goods-producing industries and production buffer stock problems for other industries were included in the commodity market responses. In this manner, regions may experience their independent cycles.

Special regional characteristics were hypothesized for government activity. In addition, labor supply equations were specified that not only conformed to household utility maximizing behavior, but also permitted factor price equalization, in the event that commodity flows were slow to adjust to interregional price differences. Of course, the proof of the model is in the estimation and simulation. The remaining income and price relationships need to be specified, and several accounting relationships are needed, to fit the behavioral structure into available data. Then, the above, more generalized, hypothesis of regional labor market behavior will be ready for confirmation or refutation.

NOTATION EMPLOYED

CI	Commercial and industrial loans
CPI	Consumer price index
d	Depreciation rate

E	Employment
FED	Federal civilian employment
H	Production worker workweek
IL	Installment loans
K	Construction stock
L	Labor input
LF	Labor force
LQ	Location quotient
Mil	Number of military personnel
MIG	Migration
MO	Mortgages outstanding
NLI	Nonlabor income
NP	Nonproduction workers
OLI	Other labor income
P	Product price
Pop	Population
PQ	Current value of output
Q	Physical output
r	Interest rate
$r - pe$	Measure of real interest rate
RPI	Real personal income
RT	Activity in retail trade
S	Sales
SUP	Supplementary wage income of state and local government employees
t	Time
TREV	Total revenues
ULC	Unit labor costs
UNEM	Unemployment rate
VA	Value-added in state and local government
w	Hourly labor cost
W	Average annual wage earnings per worker
WB	Total wage bill
WBill	Wage bill
WBP	Wage disbursements to production workers
WMIN	Variable reflecting minimum wage
WTAX	Payroll tax paid by employees

In general, subscripts refer to individual industries. Superscript R refers to the region, while superscript US refers to the nation. Similarly, a superscript e refers to an expected value, while a $*$ denotes an equilibrium value. A line over a variable name denotes a normal previous peak value.

NOTES

1. A variable to measure the different cyclical responsiveness of industries in different states was incorporated in the regional models distributed by Chase Econometrics.
2. These have been most extensively utilized by Norman Glickman (especially 1971, 1977).
3. For example, see R.J. Anderson, Jr. (1970).
4. Especially J. M. Rodgers (1973) and D. Greytak (1969).
5. C. Blanco (1963, 1964).
6. See D. Ratajczak (1974).
7. This procedure for estimating other than equilibrium demand for labor inputs was introduced by R.C. Fair (1969).
8. An extensive literature has been generated concerning the interrelationship between personnel and production decisions, beginning with the important articles by G.A. Hay (1970) and R.C. Fair (1974).
9. The difference between notional and effective demand was first presented by R.W. Clower (1965) and has since been popularized by Robert Barro and Herschel Grossman (1976). In essence, the notional demand is the equilibrium condition that would exist in a market if all other relevant markets were also in equilibrium.
10. The log (W/P) variable in equation (6.1) becomes $log\ (W/\mathrm{LQ}_{-a} \times P)$ or $log\ (W/P) + log\ (1/\mathrm{LQ}_{-a})$. After transformation, the result is $log\ W/P + a\ log\ \mathrm{LQ}$. Therefore, $b_3^6 = b_2^6 a$. As $a > 0$ and $b_2^6 < 0$, then $b_3^6 < 0$.
11. J.W. Kendrick and C.M. Jaycox (1965).
12. B.T. McCallum (1974).
13. This issue was addressed by J.L. Stein (1958).
14. $P^e = b \sum_{i=1}^{n} P_{t-1}$ where P_{t-i} is the actual price in some recent period.
15. In the simulations of economic activity in the Wharton model, which were discussed by M.K. Evans (1969), most reasonable values of an accelerator-multiplier system occurred with a five-quarter inventory cycle. See pp. 369–372.
16. Equation (6.8a) is derived by subtracting equation (6.7) for period $t - 1$ from equation (6.7) in period t to get $\mathrm{GQ}_i = log\ Q_{it} - log\ Q_{it-1}$. Arguments for inventory adjustments are included, as described earlier, in order to arrive at this specification.
17. In effect, an estimated imbalance is derived after the iterative technique has determined parameters from which estimates of desired concentrations of government employment are determined. Then TREV is increased until b_4 TREV is sufficiently large to explain the imbalance. This enhanced TREV is the $\overline{\mathrm{TREV}}$ in equation (6.17a).
18. This follows the procedure of S.W. Black and H.H. Kelejian (1970).
19. This reflects the labor-consumption decisions made by households, e.g., R. C. Fair (1974), chapter 4.
20. D. Ratajczak (1974).

II APPLICATIONS

7 IMPACT ANALYSIS WITH REGIONAL ECONOMETRIC MODELS

Norman J. Glickman*

7.1 INTRODUCTION

The purpose of this paper is to set out the uses of regional econometric models for economic impact analysis. By impact analysis, I mean the problem of analyzing and forecasting the ramifications of exogenous shocks to regional economic systems. Such shocks might come from changes in ex-regional economic policy (such as stimulative or deflationary fiscal or monetary policy), more specific ex-regional spending decisions (changes in federal government spending, such as the closing of a defense facility), and other related types of phenomena. Through the use of regional econometric models, analysts can capture the direct and indirect effects on regions. For further treatment of this subject, see Klein and Glickman (1977), Glickman (1974), and L'Esperance (1976).

I will use as my major example the experience with the Philadelphia Region Econometric Model (outlined completely in Glickman, 1977), a large-scale model of the Philadelphia SMSA. The model has 228 time series variables (using both annual and quarterly series), including output and

*Associate Professor of City and Regional Planning, University of Pennsylvania.

employment (for nineteen industrial sectors), wages, prices, and income, retail sales, manufacturing investment, banking, federal and local government, demographic and consumption. In addition, the City of Philadelphia is broken out separately for modeling purposes, and the suburban subregion is also given within the model. Since 1973, we have undertaken a series of tests of the model and carried out a wide-ranging set of forecasting and other policy-related exercises. This paper sets out some of the results of this work, with particular emphasis on impact analysis.

7.2 THEORETICAL NOTIONS

The general form of the model is given in equation (7.1):

$$\beta y_t + \Gamma z_t = u_t \tag{7.1}$$

where:

β = a nonsingular $G \times G$ matrix of coefficients of the endogenous variables;

y_t = a vector of G endogenous variables in period t;

Γ = a $G \times K$ matrix of coefficients of the exogenous variables;

z_t = a vector of K exogenous variables in period t; and

u_t = a vector of G random errors in period t, assumed to have zero means and a constant covariance matrix Σ; also assumed to be nonautocorrelated.

From the structural form of equation (7.1), we can solve for the *reduced form* of the model in equation (7.2):

$$y_t = \Lambda z_t + v_t \tag{7.2}$$

where:

$$\Lambda = -\beta^{-1}\Gamma$$
$$v_t = \beta^{-1}u_t$$

Given equation (7.2), one can then test the model's properties in several ways. The most usual one is to simulate the model over the sample period. Given the starting values of the endogenous variables, the coefficients (Λ), and the actual values of the exogenous variables ($z_1, \ldots, z_t$), one may calculate a set of predicted endogenous variables ($\tilde{y}_t$) and compare them with the actual values (y). In the case of a nonlinear model, it is not generally possible to directly calculate the reduced form; thus, numerical methods, such as the Gauss-Siedel iterative technique, must be used to approximate the reduced form.

The major problem in the evaluation of sample period performance is the absence of standardized statistical tests to gauge performance; this is in contradistinction to the single equation case, where there is a well-developed body of literature involving hypothesis testing. One may calculate the Mean Absolute Percent Error (MAPE), the Root Mean Square Error (RMSE), or Theil's "U" coefficient for multiequation systems, but these do not carry the weight of single-equation tests. Therefore, one may be able to compare the results of MAPE or RMSE statistics with the results obtained by various authors, but with no standardized statistical tests. Such was done with the Philadelphia Model, and the results have been reported in Glickman (1977, chapter 4). Some 60 percent of the Mean Absolute Percent Error statistics — a commonly used measure of model fit — were less than 3 percent.

Another set of model tests involved shocks to the system. As shown by Goldberger (1959) and Theil and Boot (1962), "impact" and "total" multipliers can be calculated by shocking the entire equation system. Thus, one calculates a *control solution* involving the analyst's "best guess" as to the future course of the exogenous variables:

$$y_T^c, y_{T+1}^c, y_{T+2}^c, \ldots \ldots y_{T+k}^c \tag{7.3}$$

and then a *perturbed solution* in which one or more exogenous variables is shocked by the amount ∂:

$$y_T^p, y_{T+1}^p, y_{T+2}^p, \ldots \ldots y_{T+k}^p. \tag{7.4}$$

One is then able to calculate a *dynamic multiplier* of the form:

$$\frac{y_{T+k}^p - y_{T+k}^c}{\partial} \tag{7.5}$$

Since the interpretation of multipliers is complicated by the fact that the multiplier's size is a function of the units of both the endogenous and exogenous variables, it is helpful to calculate instead the impact elasticity, which transforms the multipliers so as to make interpretation easier.

In order to investigate the model's dynamic properties, the Philadelphia model was shocked by 1 percent increases in all of the regional exogenous variables (tax rates, intergovernmental revenues, welfare expenditures, etc.) and national exogenous variables (Gross National Product, total manufacturing output, output in national industries by sector, transfer payments, federal government purchases, etc.). Given a once and for all shock to the model, the elasticities were calculated, and are summarized for important variables in table 7–1.

First, the regional exogenous variables were altered; their impacts on the model over time are shown in the first three columns of table 7–1. There, Gross Regional Output has a 0.123 percent response to a 1 percent change in

Table 7–1. Impact elasticities of shocks to the region from national and regional exogenous forces

	Regional exogenous			National exogenous			All exogenous		
	Year 1	Year 3	Year 8	Year 1	Year 3	Year 8	Year 1	Year 3	Year 8
Output, Gross Regional Product	0.123	0.189	0.211	0.73	1.04	1.23	0.85	1.23	1.44
Output, manufacturing, total	0.059	0.081	0.087	1.21	1.42	1.44	1.27	1.50	1.52
Output, nonmanufacturing, total	0.161	0.253	0.292	0.44	0.82	1.12	0.60	1.07	1.41
Personal income, total	0.198	0.277	0.319	0.38	0.81	1.21	0.58	1.09	1.55
Total personal income	0.182	0.251	0.290	0.23	0.62	0.99	0.41	0.87	1.28
Employment, total	0.211	0.303	0.364	0.21	0.66	1.12	0.42	0.96	1.48
Employment, manufacturing, total	0.259	0.295	0.323	0.53	1.18	1.81	0.79	1.48	2.13
Employment, nonmanufacturing, total	0.194	0.305	0.378	0.10	0.47	0.87	0.29	0.77	1.25
Philadelphia City, employment, total	0.017	0.030	0.038	0.54	0.92	1.06	0.55	0.95	1.09
Suburban, employment, total	0.316	0.449	0.539	0.04	0.51	1.13	0.35	0.96	1.67
Philadelphia City, personal income total	0.173	0.244	0.282	0.42	0.86	1.23	0.60	1.11	1.51

the regional exogenous variables during the first period. This impact increases to 0.189 percent in the third period and to 0.211 percent by the eighth period; thus, about 58 percent of the shock to Gross Regional Output (0.123/0.211) is felt in the first year, and 90 percent after three years. Similarly, we see that, in most other cases, between 60–70 percent of the entire shock is indicated within the first three years, 50–60 percent during the first year. Overall, nonmanufacturing activity (output and employment in non-manufacturing) showed greater response to the shocks from the regional exogenous variables than did manufacturing variables. This is not surprising, since these are locally-oriented activities and should be expected to respond to regional shocks.

Next, each of the national exogenous variables was shocked; see columns 4–6 of table 7–1. Here, also as expected, the response of the export-oriented manufacturing activity is greater than that for nonmanufacturing. For example, output in manufacturing has a large initial elasticity of 1.21, as opposed to 0.44 for nonmanufacturing output; ultimately, the elasticities are 1.44 and 1.12 respectively. Thus, first-year response in the manufacturing sector was approximately 85 percent of the ultimate impact. On the other hand, since the impact on the export sector spreads to the local sector with a lag, nonmanufacturing output first responds mildly (showing only 39 percent of its ultimate response in the first year), but builds up rapidly over time.

In the last three columns of table 7–1, we see the total impact of a 1 percent change in all exogenous variables. The figures in these columns show that the region responds much more to shocks in national variables, and therefore changes in national growth, than in relation to changes in regional activity. Note also that there is a greater response from suburban variables than from those in Philadelphia City for the combined national and regional shocks.

7.3 FORECASTING AND POLICY SIMULATIONS WITH THE PHILADELPHIA ECONOMETRIC MODEL

The standard method employed in making forecasts with regional econometric models is to set equation (7.2)'s error term v equal to zero and assume that the estimate of the reduced form (Λ) coefficients are unchanged from the sample to forecast periods. Thus, to make forecasts using a linear model, we have for the kth forecast period:

$$y_{T+k} = \Lambda z_{T+k} \tag{7.6}$$

With a nonlinear model such as the Philadelphia Econometric Model, even though numerical methods must be used to approximate the reduced form, the assumption about Λ and v remain the same. Such short-term and long-term forecasts have also been reported in Glickman (1977, chapter 4). The record of the model is reasonably good.

7.3.1 Impact of the Oil Shortage

Policy simulations involving various shocks to the model can also be described. For instance, in 1973 we attempted to set out the impact of the so-called "oil crisis" on the region. Here we worked in a two-stage process, as is the usual procedure. First, the Wharton Industry and Long-Term Model ("WILT") (Preston, 1972) was used to make a "shocked" solution for the national economy. Then the regional model, using the "shocked" values of the national model, was used to make forecasts. But this was not a mechanical routine. Additional (noneconometric model) regional analysis was undertaken because of the nature of the region's economy.

In the national forecast, two assumptions were made regarding the importation of oil. As is well known, the import deficit had a significant effect on the American economy over the short- and, perhaps, long term. Under the assumption of a two million barrel per day import deficit for 1974, the WILT model showed a national growth of GNP of only 0.5 percent for 1974 and 2.7 percent for 1975. The national rate of unemployment was expected to rise from the late-1973 level of 4.7 percent to 5.5 percent in 1974 and 6.4 percent in 1975; this was to be accomplished by a marked decrease in capital utilization over this period. There were to be particularly strong and negative impacts upon the steel and chemical industries nationally, as well as on the petroleum sector.

The impact of the oil deficit was felt significantly in the Philadelphia region because there is a major concentration of oil refinery capacity in the region, about 60 percent of the total on the east coast of the United States. Significantly, this capacity is largely used for the refining of imported oil, especially oil from the Middle East. In addition, the region's industrial base is heavily dependent upon oil since there is considerable chemical and steel activity in the Philadelphia area. An analysis of this impact was undertaken, using the Philadelphia input-output table (Isard et al., 1967) and information obtained from local businessmen to gauge the differential impact on the region. In columns 2 and 3 of table 7–2, the growth of the Philadelphia region, under the assumption of a 2-million barrel per day oil deficit, is shown: Gross Regional Output was expected to grow by 0.44 percent in

Table 7-2. Impact of the oil shortage on the region

	Alternative 1: Two million b/d import deficit			Alternative 2: Three million b/d import deficit	
	(1) 1973	(2) 1974	(3) 1975	(4) 1974	(5) 1975
Output, Gross					
National Product	21736.00	21831.00	22437.00	21480.00	21945.00
(percent change)	7.03	0.44	2.77	− 1.18	2.16
Output, manufacturing,					
total	8067.00	8052.00	8361.00	7927.00	8198.00
Output, nonmanufacturing,					
total	13670.00	13799.00	14076.00	13553.00	13747.00
Employment, total	2066.00	2091.00	2113.00	2080.00	2079.00
(percent change)	1.20	1.20	1.02	0.66	− 0.02
Employment, manufacturing,					
total	544.00	551.00	564.00	544.00	546.00
Employment, nonmanufacturing,					
total	1523.00	1541.00	1549.00	1536.00	1534.00
Total personal income					
(current values)	25619.00	27626.00	30176.00	27412.00	29570.00
(percent change)	7.21	7.83	9.23	6.66	7.87
Total personal income					
(real values)	15992.00	15919.00	16041.00	15742.00	15635.00
(percent change)	− 0.75	− 0.46	0.76	− 1.87	− 0.68
Unemployment rate	5.20	5.94	6.30	6.37	7.18
Consumer Price Index	160.20	173.53	188.12	174.13	189.12
(percent change)	8.02	8.32	8.40	8.70	8.61

1974 and 2.77 percent in 1975; Total employment was forecasted to expand at a constant rate of 1.20 percent from 1973 to 1974, with the rate of increase dropping to 1.02 percent in 1975. Personal income grew at reasonably healthy rates, but, due to inflation, there was a −0.46 percent fall in real Personal Income in 1974. The rate of unemployment rose to 5.9 percent in 1974 and 6.3 percent in 1975.

In columns 4 and 5 we show the impact of a three million barrel per day oil import deficit on the region, the amount forecasted by the National Petroleum Council and included in the Wharton forecast. Under this set of assumptions, the national economy was expected to go into a recession in 1974, with unemployment rising to 5.6 percent in 1974 and 6.3 percent in 1975. Again the impact on Philadelphia was more severe: Gross Regional

Output should fall by 1.18 percent in 1974, and the rate of unemployment should increase to 6.3 percent. Personal income growth would be 6.7 percent (compared to 7.8 percent under the 2-million barrel per day solution), and this, in real terms, would be a −1.87 percent fall. The oil shortage also caused the increased inflation. Thus, the impact on the Philadelphia region was quite substantial over the shortrun, given the current situation involving energy deficits.

Thus, the procedure for making an impact study is as follows.

1. A forecast of the national economy is made; in our case we used the Wharton Model for this.
2. Forecasts of the regional exogenous variables are made; various methods may be used for this.
3. The analyst makes some nonmodel analysis of the particular region under study (this is not always the case).
4. The regional econometric model is simulated, given the assumptions and adjustments noted above.

This is the manner in which we at the University of Pennsylvania and Wharton-EFA undertake our modeling efforts. Other simulations are noted below.

7.3.2 The Impact of Revenue-sharing on the Region

It is interesting to examine the impact of federal revenue-sharing on the Philadelphia region. Intergovernmental revenues enter the model through several equations. We were able, therefore, to change levels of these revenues and see the differential impact on Philadelphia. The model was shocked with an increase of approximately 109 million dollars in federal revenue-sharing funds — 10 percent more than in the base year — and column 1 of table 7–3 shows the initial impact of revenue-sharing. A 10 percent increase in these variables results in, approximately, a 6 percent increase in Gross Regional Output and approximately a 3 percent increase in Employment and Personal Income in the region.

As expected, the major impact comes in the sector on government activity. For instance, municipal government total revenues increase 38 percent and tax revenues increase 4.8 percent; for school districts, the impact on total revenues is greater: there is a 43 percent increase in the initial year for total revenues. Since, in the model, levels of expenditures are in part a function of the levels of revenues, then it follows that the expenditure variables

Table 7–3.   The impact of revenue-sharing on the region

Variables	Elasticity		Absolute impact*	
	Year 1	Sum of eight years	Year 1	Sum of eight years
Output, Gross				
Regional Product	0.0573	0.1154	125.496	260.039
Employment,				
total	0.0287	0.1225	6.017	26.193
Personal income,				
total	0.0327	0.1119	90.027	345.484
Municipal government,				
total expenditures	0.2528	0.4337	39.170	70.511
Municipal government,				
total revenues	0.3806	0.4325	54.326	62.794
Municipal government,				
tax revenues	0.0481	0.1284	4.466	12.994
School districts,				
total expenditures	0.4248	0.6611	61.981	99.969
School districts,				
total revenues	0.4303	0.6693	61.827	99.611
School districts,				
tax revenues	0.0260	0.4289	2.187	39.971
Philadelphia City,				
personal income,				
total	0.0284	0.0993	37.762	146.043
Philadelphia City,				
municipal government,	0.3287	0.3532	26.768	29.051
total expenditures				
Philadelphia City,				
municipal government,	0.4214	0.4445	33.417	35.536
total revenues				
Philadelphia City,				
municipal government,	0.0118	0.0483	0.607	2.726
tax revenues				
Philadelphia City,				
school district,	0.4367	0.5125	22.641	27.445
total expenditures				
Philadelphia City,				
school district,	0.6128	0.6568	28.780	31.205
total revenues				
Federal income tax				
paid by residents	0.0357	0.1231	10.056	38.591

*Dollar and employment variables in thousands

will also be affected by this shock to the revenue side. This simulation shows that municipal expenditures increase the initial year by 25 percent, and school expenditures by 42 percent. The impact is similarly felt on the Philadelphia City subsector, as the major revenue variables and private sector variables (such as personal income) increase in a manner commensurate with the region.

As expected, the shock to the model builds up over time, and, in column 2 of table 7-3, the total impact of the 10 percent increase in revenue sharing in the region is shown. For example, the ultimate increases in Gross Regional Output, Employment, and Personal Income are approximately 11-12 percent. The impact on the government variables is also significant: total municipal revenues increase by some 43 percent, and school revenues by nearly 67 percent, when the full effects to the system as a whole are felt. In the Philadelphia City subsector, similar results obtain.

Columns 3 and 4 indicate the dollar value and employment effects in absolute terms on the region. Thus, in the long run, a $109 million increase in intergovernmental revenues will lead to a $260 million increase in real Gross Output and a $345.5 million increase in Personal income.

Most interesting for our analysis is that total revenues for municipalities and school districts increased by approximately $162.4 million versus the initial shock of $109 million; thus, the growth of the region due to the effects of additional federal funds leads to greater amounts of government spending by the amount of $53.4 million. Of additional import is the impact of revenue-sharing on the social accounts of the region versus the federal government. The $109 million increment in intergovernmental revenues leads to an increase of $38.6 million in federal income taxes paid by residents of the region. In addition, since Gross Output increases by $260.0 million in real terms and $510.6 million in money terms (not shown in table 7-3), increased corporate income taxes paid by corporations in the region also help to offset the initial expenditure by the federal government in the Philadelphia region.

7.3.3 Balancing Philadelphia City Government Budget

As with other large central cities, Philadelphia City has experienced serious fiscal problems, especially long-term deficits on the current account. Our 1981 control solution (shown in Panel A of table 7-4) indicates that, given the current assumptions about the property tax and wage tax rates, the city will continue to have significant deficits. Starting in 1975 we saw a $28 million deficit on the current account, which grows to some $85 million by 1980.

Table 7-4. Balancing the Philadelphia City government budget (dollar figures in millions, tax rates in percent)

A. Control solution	1975	1976	1977	1978	1979	1980
Total expenditures	790.00	847.00	908.00	973.00	1040.00	1111.00
Total revenues	762.00	834.00	881.00	928.00	976.00	1026.00
Property tax rate	2.37	2.50	2.50	2.50	2.50	2.50
Wage tax rate	3.16	3.50	3.50	3.50	3.50	3.50
Expenditures minus revenues	(28.00)	(13.00)	(27.00)	(45.00)	(64.00)	(85.00)

B. Alternative solution 1: Property tax increase	1975	1976	1977	1978	1979	1980
Total expenditures	792.00	849.00	911.00	976.00	1044.00	1115.00
Total revenues	796.00	851.00	917.00	984.00	1050.00	1120.00
Property tax rate	3.02	3.00	3.25	3.50	3.75	4.15
Wage tax rate	3.16	3.50	3.50	3.50	3.50	3.50
Expenditures minus revenues	(4.00)	2.00	6.00	8.00	6.00	5.00

C. Alternative solution 2: Wage tax increase	1975	1976	1977	1978	1979	1980
Total expenditures	792.00	849.00	911.00	976.00	1043.00	1115.00
Total revenues	789.00	848.00	911.00	976.00	1041.00	1115.00
Property tax rate	2.37	2.50	2.50	2.50	2.50	2.50
Wage tax rate	3.86	4.00	4.25	4.50	4.75	5.25
Expenditures minus revenues	(3.00)	(1.00)	0.00	0.00	(2.00)	0.00

D. Alternative solution 3: Property and wage tax increase	1975	1976	1977	1978	1979	1980
Total expenditures	792.00	849.00	911.00	976.00	1044.00	1115.00
Total revenues	795.00	852.00	911.00	985.00	1052.00	1124.00
Property tax rate	2.63	2.70	2.78	2.92	3.02	3.20
Wage tax rate	3.62	3.84	3.94	4.16	4.33	4.60
Expenditures minus revenues	3.00	3.00	0.00	11.00	8.00	9.00

Another type of impact analysis may be seen as we examine various methods of altering levels of the property tax or the wage tax in order to produce a balanced budget. In Panel B of table 7-4, we manipulate the property tax only. It is shown there that the tax rate must be increased from the current 2.37 percent to 3.02 percent in 1975 and 4.15 percent in 1980, assuming that the wage tax does not change. In Panel C the property tax is held constant at control solution levels and the wage tax is increased. It is seen that the wage tax must increase 5.25 percent, the property tax held constant, if the municipal budget is to be balanced. Finally, in Panel D we assume that both the property and wage taxes can be increased, and we see that the 1980 mix will be a 4.60 percent rate for the wage tax. Both are significantly higher than the 2.50 percent and 3.50 percent levels projected by our control solution for the two taxes, respectively.

7.3.4 The Impact of Defense Spending

Philadelphia is a major center for defense procurement in the northeastern United States. Located in the region are the Defense Industrial Supply Center, the Army Electronics Command, the Frankford Arsenal, and the Philadelphia Naval Base, among other facilities. It was announced in 1974 that significant cuts in spending and employment would be made for many of these activity centers.

To gauge the impacts of the projected $100 million reduction in defense spending, a simulation of this policy was carried out by making constant adjustments in the federal employment, defense spending, and federal output equations. In addition, spending was reduced in the manufacturing and nonmanufacturing industries where there would be the most impact; information on the industrial breakdown of direct federal defense-related expenditures is available from the input-output study by Isard and Langford (1969).

The results of this simulation experiment are shown in table 7-5. The major impact of the defense-spending reduction, assumed to occur in 1975, is felt immediately. Thus, $94.9 million of direct impact is recorded in 1975, out of a total impact of $161.3 million after eight years. Consistent with previous simulations, a large proportion of the total impact in manufacturing is felt immediately, nearly 80 percent in the first year. Once again, the impact on nonmanufacturing is relatively minor at the outset, but builds to a total of $99.9 million after eight years. Total impact on employment in the region is some 13,000 jobs lost over the eight-year period, 2,500 immediately. A total of $289.7 million is lost in personal income, of which $135 million is in real terms. Thus, the impact on the region is quite significant.

Table 7-5. Impact of defense-spending reductions on the region: $100 million (all dollar figures in millions) (employment figures in thousands)

	1975	Total impact
Gross Regional Output	$94.9	161.3
Output, manufacturing, total	$48.5	61.3
Output, nonmanufacturing, total	$46.3	99.9
Employment, total	2.487	13.260
Employment, manufacturing, total	1.460	5.617
Employment, nonmanufacturing, total	1.027	7.643
Personal income, total (current values)	$132.6	289.7
Total personal income (real values)	$63.2	134.7
Philadelphia City, personal income, total	$55.7	122.5
Suburban, personal income, total	$76.8	167.2

7.4 CONCLUSION

In this brief review, I have shown some of the ways in which regional econometric models can be used to gauge the impact of external economic events. Some of the simulations described are simple, but the methodology is solid and should be clear to all. Econometric models can be used to calculate multipliers or elasticities in a flexible and cost-effective way.

It is important to understand that more interesting impact analyses can be undertaken if more detailed and disaggregated regional econometric models are built in the future. I note here the particular importance of devising more detailed public sectors in econometric models. Most models built to date do not go very far in this direction. The growth and refinement of regional econometric models will provide the detail to make significantly more interesting impact studies.

8 THE ROLE OF INPUT-OUTPUT MODELS IN REGIONAL IMPACT ANALYSIS

William A. Schaffer*

8.1 INTRODUCTION

"Impact analysis" is the most frequently suggested use of regional input-output models. This paper outlines approaches to impact analysis used in two studies with which the author has been involved: the Georgia input-output study, and a study of the impact of the Montreal Expos.[1] The paper has four parts: an outline of a simple regional model, to establish a starting point; a review of the place of structural change in input-output analysis; a discussion of the development-simulation technique used in Georgia; and, finally, an illustration of impact analysis in Montreal.

8.2 A REGIONAL INPUT-OUTPUT MODEL

The typical regional input-output model is based on a transactions table that can be described in terms of two equations systems. The first identifies the disposition of regionally produced industry outputs as follows:

$$\sum_{j=1}^{s} x_{ij} + \sum_{f=1}^{t} y_{if} + e_i = x_i \ (i = 1,2,3, \ldots s) \tag{8.1}$$

*Professor of Economics, Georgia Institute of Technology.

where

x_{ij} = sales of regional industry i to regional industry j,
y_{if} = sales of regional industry i to regional final demand sector f,
e_i = export sales of regional industry i,
x_i = total sales of regional industry i,
s = dimension of the input-output matrix, and
t = the number of final demand sectors, excluding exports.

The second equation system defines industry purchases as

$$\sum_{i=1}^{s} x_{ij} + \sum_{p=1}^{t} v_{pj} + \sum_{i=1}^{s} m_{ij} +$$

$$\sum_{k=1}^{v} n_{kj} = x_j \; (j = 1,2,3, \ldots s) \qquad (8.2)$$

where

v_{pj} = value added by final-payment sector p in industry j,
m_{ij} = imports by industry j of the products competitive to industry i, and
n_{kj} = imports of the product of noncompetitive industry k.

As is well known, the system is solved by assuming a constant production relation such that

$$x_{ij} = a_{ij} \cdot x_j \qquad (8.3)$$

and then substituting equation (8.3) into equation (8.1), thus reducing the number of unknowns to equality with the number of equations:

$$\sum_{i=1}^{s} a_{ij} \cdot x_j + \sum_{f=1}^{t} y_{if} + e_i = x_i (i = 1,2,3, \ldots s) \qquad (8.4)$$

In matrix notation, this system can be represented as

$$A \cdot X + Y_\iota + E = X, \qquad (8.5)$$

with capital letters indicating matrices and vectors of the elements defined above, and ι representing a vector of ones, used for summing. Its solution becomes

$$B \cdot (Y_\iota + E) = X, \qquad (8.6)$$

where B is $(I - A)^{-1}$. Here b_{ij} represents the direct and indirect purchases from industry i by industry j in satisfying one additional unit of final demand.

The A matrix is frequently closed with respect to households by the addition of the household row $(v_{1j}, \; j = 1,2,3, \ldots s+1)$ and the household column $(y_{i1}, i = 1,2,3,\ldots s)$ to the regional transactions matrix (the x_{ij}'s). When this augmented matrix is used, elements of the inverse represent the direct, indirect, and induced purchases from industry i by industry j in satisfying one additional unit of the remaining final demand. The term "induced" derives from "purchases induced by household consumption."

8.3 ECONOMIC CHANGE IN INPUT-OUTPUT MODELS

In input-output analysis, economic change can take two forms — structural change or change in final demand. Change in the economic structure of a region can take place in several ways. It might occur through private investment in the new production facilities, through other technological change, through changes in the marketing structure of the economy, or through public investment in such social capital as schools, highways, river systems, parks, etc. Changes in final demand are primarily changes in demands by other areas, investors, or governments for the goods produced in the region. Let us now put these in the context of our model.

8.3.1 Structural Change

Structural change can be interpreted as *changes in regional production coefficients*. These changes have two sources: changes in technology or changes in marketing patterns. With a regional production coefficient written as

$$a_{ij} = p_{ij} \cdot r_{ij}, \tag{8.7}$$

these changes can be easily illustrated. The technical production coefficient, p_{ij}, shows the proportion of inputs purchased from industry i by industry j, without regard to location of industry i; the regional trade coefficient, r_{ij}, shows the proportion of that purchase made within the region.

A change in technology could be illustrated by a shift from mechanical weeding to chemical weeding in agriculture, from glass bottles to metal cans in the soft-drink industry, or from oil to coal for industrial fuel needs. This is a restrictive interpretation of technological change, in that it involves changes in current flows. We do not normally or easily trace either changes in capital intensity or technological changes embodied in capital equipment through input-output models. The initial impact of a change in capital intensity — new construction or equipment expenditure — might be traced through an input-output system as a change in final demand. And to the extent that technological change can be viewed primarily as facilitating a change in capacity and, therefore, in export sales, the impact of the change can be traced. But regional input-output models are not normally constructed with such finely detailed coefficients that changes in incomes accruing to capital and labor can be identified with great confidence. Technological changes in the broad sense are related to the dynamic questions of economic growth, and so are not amenable to analysis through a static model.

A change in import patterns, or a change in r_{ij}, would be illustrated by a shift from imported to locally produced weeding devices, by a move of a metal-can producer into the region, or by the reopening of a local coal mine.

The above changes are phrased in terms of the existing plant structure. In addition, change can occur through the introduction of a new plant into the region. This form of change also involves changes in regional production coefficients, but the change occurs over an entire column of coefficients rather than in just a few sets.

The way in which a new plant is introduced into an input-output system depends in large part on the aggregation scheme employed. Assume that our classificatory scheme is exhaustive and shows the manufacturing activities in our diversified and industrialized region in major-industry-group detail. The transportation equipment industry includes several auto and truck assembly plants, as well as an aircraft plant. The introduction of a second aircraft producer would increase the weights of aircraft coefficients in forming the coefficient of the aggregated transportation equipment industry, and so would cause structural change as expressed above. (Actually, such a shift in coefficients could be caused by a simple change in product mix within the aggregated industry.)

New plants can also be handled as completely new industries. The introduction of a new plant — an oil refinery, for example — which is the only representative of its industry group, would require that we add another row and column to the input-output table.

The smoothness with which we are able to handle structural changes involving new plants depends as much on our worksheets as on available data. A fairly detailed set of worksheets permits the analyst to reweight coefficient for a particular industry, or even to isolate them if separate treatment is helpful. These problems are discussed later in this paper.

8.3.2 Change in Final Demand

Accounting for structural change requires great familiarity with the details of an input-output table. This is not the case when accounting for the effect of final demand changes, a task which normally can be accomplished with only the Leontief inverse in hand. Indeed, the reason for establishing lengthy tables of multipliers is to facilitate use of input-output models in tracing the effects of these simple changes.

The multipliers can take a variety of forms, but usually they are computed as

$$M_{pj} = \sum_i b_{ij} \cdot v_{pi} \qquad (8.8)$$

where the subscript p determines the kind of multiplier. By using the different p elements of value-added expressed as proportions of output (v_{pi}), we can create multipliers for personal income, local government revenues, and state government revenues. By substituting employment (W_j) for v_{pi}, we can develop employment multipliers. And, by letting v_{pi} equal 1 for all industries, we can produce output multipliers.[2] When the A matrix includes only industrial sectors, direct and indirect effects are traced through the system; when it also includes the household sector, direct, indirect, and induced effects are traced. Although tradition labels these as Type I and Type II multipliers, I prefer the terms "simple" and "total," as more descriptive.

These multipliers permit us to identify the total impacts on incomes, output, and employment of a change in final demand. If we wish more detail regarding the specific industries in which changes will occur, we can work with the elements of the inverse itself to obtain:

$$D_i = \sum_j b_{ij} \cdot \Delta e_j \qquad (i = 1, 2, \ldots n), \qquad (8.9)$$

where Δe_j is change in final demand for industry j, and D_i is total change in the output of industry i due to Δe_j. These D_i may then be multiplied by the v_{pi} above to show changes in the various industries.

8.4 SIMULATING DEVELOPMENT IN GEORGIA

In the Georgia input-output system, we developed a set of procedures for simulating the introduction of a new plant or industry into the economy.[3] These procedures take advantage of the data system on which the Georgia table is based, and apply the various multipliers to expected changes.

The Georgia input-output table is defined in the same terms as is the U.S. table. In worksheet detail, its interindustry transactions are for 300 of the 367 detailed industries used in the national scheme; the remaining 67 industries do not exist within the state, and so are "noncompetitive." In establishing our initial estimates, we used a price-adjusted version of the 1963 national table, reorganizing it to fit the Georgia economy. Survey data were collected for the manufacturing industries, and the system was modified over a series of estimates to yield a final table embodying all available data on the state.

One particularly important addition to our data was a set of final-payment ratios based on a review of over 600 corporate income tax returns by the Georgia Department of Revenue. With this data we were able to estimate values for payments by each industry to households, to a capital residual (depreciation, profits, etc.), to local governments, to state government, and to the federal government. These payments, the v_{pj} of equation (8.2), form the basis for household and government income multipliers.

8.4.1 New-Plant Simulation

To see the effect of introducing a new plant in an industry that already exists in Georgia, we developed a *new-plant simulator*. This procedure is actually a revision of our aggregation procedure. We simply specify that the Georgia input-output table be aggregated from the worksheet level to the presentation level, to include one more detailed industry. This table is then inverted, and a table like table 8-1 is produced. The columns in this table report elements from the appropriate column in this inverse, multiplied by 1 (for output); the employee-output ratio; and income-output ratios for households, local governments, and state governments, and then multiplied by a postulated increase in industry output due to the new plant. That is, they are $b_{ij} v_{pj} \cdot \Delta e_j$, where industry j is the subject of investigation. The sum of each column is the appropriate multiplier times the postulated output change.

8.4.2 New-Industry Simulation

To see the effect of a plant in an entirely new industry, a more complex procedure must be followed. A set of new coefficients must be developed and inserted into the table.

In the Georgia system, we developed these coefficients from the detailed national table. The rows and columns for the sixty-seven noncompetitive industries were retained in price-adjusted form. The columns provided the technical coefficients for new industries. We used the average regional trade coefficient for each of its supplying industries to reduce these technical coefficients to regional terms.

For the row representing the new industry, we used purchases from our worksheets, with an estimate of trade based on the supply-demand pool

Table 8–1. Changes in the Georgia economy resulting from an additional $5.000 million plant in the veneer and plywood industry (millions of dollars)

	Output value	Output percent	Change due to new plant in Number of employees	Personal income	City and county revenue	State revenue
Agriculture (SIC01, 07-9)	.2	.0	0.	.1	.0	.0
Mining (SIC 10-4)	.0	.0	0.	.0	.0	.0
Contract construction (SIC 15-7)	.6	.0	0.	.1	.0	.0
Food and kindred products (SIC 20-1)	.3	.0	5.	.0	.0	.0
Textile mill products (SIC 22)	.0	.0	1.	.0	.0	.0
Apparel and related products (SIC 23)	.0	.0	2.	.0	.0	.0
Lumber and wood products (SIC 24)	.7	.2	33.	.2	.0	.0
Furniture and fixtures (SIC 25)	.0	.0	1.	.0	.0	.0
Paper and allied products (SIC 26)	.0	.0	1.	.0	.0	.0
Printing and publishing (SIC 27)	.0	.0	2.	.0	.0	.0
Chemicals and allied products (SIC 28)	.1	.0	1.	.0	.0	.0
Petroleum refining (SIC 29)	.0	.0	0.	.0	.0	.0
Rubber and miscellaneous plastics (SIC 30)	.0	.0	0.	.0	.0	.0
Leather and leather products (SIC 31)	.0	.0	0.	.0	.0	.0

Stone, clay and glass products (SIC 32)	.0	.0	1.	.0	.0	.0
Primary metal industries (SIC 33)	.0	.0	0.	.0	.0	.0
Fabricated metal products (SIC 34, 19)	.0	.0	1.	.0	.0	.0
Machinery, except electrical (SIC 35)	.0	.0	1.	.0	.0	.0
Electrical machinery & equipment (SIC 36)	.0	.0	0.	.0	.0	.0
Transportation equipment (SIC 37)	.1	.0	0.	.0	.0	.0
Miscellaneous manufacturing (SIC 38-9)	.0	.0	0.	.0	.0	.0
Transportation services (SIC 40-7)	.2	.0	10.	.1	.0	.0
Communications & utilities (SIC 48-9)	.3	.0	8.	.1	.1	.1
Wholesale and retail trade (SIC 50-9)	1.0	.0	70.	.5	.0	.0
Finance, insurance, real estate (SIC 60-7)	.8	.0	14.	.4	.0	.0
Services (SIC 70-9, 80-6, 89)	.8	.0	32.	.3	.0	.0
Government enterprises	.1	.0	0.	.0	.0	.0
Unallocated industries	.1	.0	0.	.0	.0	.0
Veneer and plywood	5.3	12.2	318.	2.0	.0	.0
Households	4.2	.0	0.	.0	.1	.1
Capital residual	.7	.0	0.	.0	.0	.0
City and county government	.3	.0	0.	.2	.0	.0
State government	.3	.0	0.	.1	.1	.1
Total	16.0	12.8	503.	4.2	.3	.3

technique. If this new industry produces more than is demanded locally, we supply all local needs (that is, we set the trade coefficients all equal to 1 for this row), and export the rest. If the new industry produces less, we supply local needs in proportion to availability and import the remainder.

After this work is completed at worksheet detail, we aggregate to presentation level, with the list now including the new industry, and proceed as above, producing a table similar to table 8–1.

8.5 SIMULATING BASEBALL IN MONTREAL

Another interesting application is a 1969 study of the economic impact of baseball on Montreal.[4] I had completed other studies of sports impact using an economic base model, and found myself in position to gather the necessary data just at the same time that I had developed a computer routine for constructing nonsurvey input-output models.

The input-output model used was based on the Canadian input-output table, on Montreal employment and income statistics, and on the supply-demand pool procedure for estimating regional trade. The result was a fifteen-sector model of Montreal, defined as above. Since the model itself is of little interest here, I have not included it. Table 8–2, however, does show our industry sectoring, and reports the output multipliers arising in the study.

We had two tasks. The first was to insert the baseball team as an industry. Two afternoons with the club treasurer produced columns 2 and 3 in table 8–2, the row and column which would represent the team in the input-output model as the sixteenth industry.

The second task involved identifying changes in final demand associated with the team. In 1969, this included construction expenditures (column 4) of $4.87 million, as well as expenditures by visitors to Montreal. The visitor expenditures were collected through a survey of fans. Of the 1.2 million attendance at home games in Montreal, 38 percent were from outside the metropolitan area, and 84 percent of these attributed their visits primarily to the game. The expenditures of these fans are reported in the last three columns of table 8–2.

Tracing the economic impact of the team, then, involves inserting the team as an industry into the model, and using multiplier analysis to trace attributed changes in final demand through the system.

To graphically present the idea that others in the community benefited from the presence of baseball, we found it important to trace the impact

Table 8–2.   Output multipliers, team sales and purchases, and baseball-related final expenditures

(dollars in thousands)

Industry	Output multiplier	Team sales	Team purchases	Baseball-related final expenditures			
				Construction, 1969 only	Local fans	Out-of-town visitors	Total current
Agriculture, forestry, fisheries	3.528	—	—	—	—	—	—
Mining	2.838	—	—	—	—	—	—
Food, tobacco	2.936	470	500	—	—	—	—
Textiles	4.569	—	90	68	—	—	—
Wood and furniture	3.393	—	—	17	—	—	—
Paper	3.110	—	—	—	—	—	—
Metal	3.687	—	—	14	—	—	—
Transport. and electrical equipment	4.432	—	—	501	—	—	—
Chemicals, rubber, petroleum	3.063	—	10	—	122	319	441
Other manufacturing	4.002	—	300	—	—	—	—
Construction	4.263	—	—	4,266	—	—	—
Trade and transportation	3.814	—	—	—	241	386	627
Utilities	2.332	80	20	—	—	—	—
Communications and service	3.201	200	1,350	4	865	1,559	2,423
Dummy industries	4.479	1,110	150	—	—	—	—
Major-league baseball	3.283	480	480	—	2,710	1,716	4,426
Local private inputs (households)	3.598	—	1,590	—	—	—	—
Other payments and imports	—	—	2,280	—	—	—	—
Local fans	—	2,710	—	—	—	—	—
Out-of-town visitors	—	1,720	—	—	—	—	—
Total	—	6,770	6,770	4,870	3,937	3,980	7,917

through individual industries, as in equation (8.9) above. The results of such a tracing are laid out in table 8-3. Note that baseball is second among industries in the impact felt from spending by out-of-town fans. The service sector, which includes restaurants and hotels, is the primary beneficiary of this spending.

Table 8-3. The financial impact of baseball on Montreal, by industry, 1969

| | Expenditures due to | | | | | |
| | Local fans | | Out-of-town fans | | Total | |
Industry	$ (mil)	%	$ (mil)	%	$ (mil)	%
Local households	2.82	22.2	2.94	23	5.76	23
Service	2.48	19.5	3.07	24	5.55	22
Baseball	2.94	23.2	1.83	14	4.77	19
Trade and transport	1.40	8.2	1.25	10	2.29	9
Food and beverage	.68	5.4	.63	5	1.31	5
Petroleum	.43	3.4	.67	5	1.10	4
Other industries	2.30	18.1	2.42	19	4.72	18
	12.69	100.0	12.81	100	25.50	100

8.6 CONCLUSION

This paper has identified the common means through which input-output models may be used for economic impact analysis. To illustrate these means, we have discussed procedures used with the Georgia model for simulating development, and we have briefly outlined the way in which the economic impact of an activity such as baseball may be traced through an input-output model.

In concluding this paper, a few critical comments would be appropriate. In presenting impact analyses, economists have emphasized almost exclusively the positive, benefit-producing aspects of projects under review. But we neglect a number of other important points, largely because of our models. One of these points is effects over time. Generally, our models are static, and data for future years is difficult to come by, especially when values stand a chance of going down as well as up.

Another neglected point is alternative costs. None of our traditional impact models are set up to show the sacrificial aspects of expenditures. With unconstrained systems we show flows, and even a large construction expenditure can be converted from a loss of alternatives to flows of outputs, employment, and incomes.

A third sidestep we take concerns linkages and economic growth. By concentrating on current flows as a measure of interindustry linkages, we neglect the agglomerative aspects of new industries and infrastructures. These agglomerative links are probably the more important keys to economic growth, and should be emphasized in impact research.

And finally, we find it easy to carelessly permit the indirect effects which we identify for a project to become secondary benefits in project appraisals. Since many projects with which we become involved are nationally financed, the increased incomes which we identify in input-output analyses are really redistributions of benefits which could accrue to other regions.

But despite these few critical remarks, I remain a firm believer. Regional input-output analysis remains our best tool for tracing impacts through an economic system.

NOTES

1. This paper derives much of its substance from Schaffer (1976) and Schaffer, Laurent, and Sutter (1972).
2. This statement should be qualified. If the household is included among "industries," as in calculating the extended inverse, an unusually high output multiplier is obtained, since industry output then includes household income. To avoid confusion, we should exclude the household element from the summed output multiplier (by setting the appropriate v_{ki} equal to zero).

   This point was brought to my attention by Rodney C. Jensen, whose comments are found in the *Annals of Regional Science* (November 1978). My reactions have been both to use the net concept suggested in this footnote (Schaffer and Biven, 1978), and to minimize the importance of output multipliers (Schaffer, et al., 1977). As measures of intermediate activities, output multipliers overcount by nature. We should remember that they are simply by-products of the search for the effects of final-demand changes on the use of, or payments to, primary inputs.
3. These procedures were designed after a careful review of the literature.
4. This unpublished study is available from the author.

9 THE MULTIREGIONAL, MULTI-INDUSTRY FORECASTING MODEL

Curtis C. Harris, Jr.*

9.1 INTRODUCTION

This paper describes the development of the Multiregional, Multi-Industry Forecasting (MRMI) Model and its applications to policy-related questions. The description is general since the details of the model have been published elsewhere (Harris, 1973). The results of some of the applications will be summarized since many of the applications have been done for government agencies and the results are not readily available.

9.2 BACKGROUND INFORMATION

The development of the Multiregional, Multi-Industry Forecasting Model was motivated by the need for a longrun regional forecasting model capable of making detailed forecasts, by industrial sector, for all regions in the U.S. Additional objectives for the model were that it be dynamic and capable of performing impact analysis.

*Professor of Economics, University of Maryland

The industry location approach that is the basis of this model was selected after careful consideration of the alternatives available in the mid-1960s. Both export-base and shift-share models were dismissed because of their inability to provide sufficient detail, and because they are subject to considerable error. At the time there were a number of national macroeconometric models, but very few, if any, at the regional level. On the other hand, there were a number of regional input-output models.

Regional input-output models are more appropriate for shortrun analysis when small increments in final demand are being considered. Their suitability for longrun analysis is questionable, since final demand generally cannot be predetermined or set in some exogenous way. Personal consumer expenditures and local government activities are not exogenous, but are related to the earnings that are generated by industrial output. Investment cannot be predetermined, since it is obviously related to output through the production function. Exports and nonlocal government activities are more apt to be exogenous; however, the reason these exports exist is because of the existence of the industry output.

Personal consumption and local government expenditures are often made endogenous to input-output models by augmenting the interindustry matrix to include these expenditures as an extra column with a corresponding additional income row. But this procedure has the problem of the fixed coefficients and, most importantly, a fixed relationship between importing goods and locally-produced goods. Since trade flows are a consequence of the location of production and consumption and transportation costs, these coefficients are likely to be unstable over time. In fact, all of the coefficients in the model which show the relationships among the local firms would change completely, whenever a new industry locates in the area.

9.3 THEORETICAL FRAMEWORK

The theoretical basis of the MRMI model can be found in the works of Von Thunen (1966), Weber (1929), Hotelling (1929), and more recently, Isard (1956) and Lefeber (1958). Basically, it is a general dynamic model in which industrial location decisions play a critical role.

Location rent is an important concept in the theory. Location rent per unit of industry i's output in producing region k (LR) is defined as the difference between the market price of commodity i in market region j (P), and the average variable cost of i in k (AVC), plus transport cost of shipping i from k to j (T). The average variable costs include a normal return on investment and any inherent or transactions value of land, but does not include land value that is associated with location. Location rents can also be defined as the sum of profits per unit of output (PF) and the rental value of land per unit of output (RVL). The definition of locational rent is:

$$\text{LR}_i^k = P_i^j - \text{AVC}_i^k - T_i^{kj} = \text{PF}_i^k + \text{RVL}_i^k \quad \begin{matrix} i = 1, \ldots, N \\ j,k = 1, \ldots, M. \end{matrix} \quad (9.1)$$

The marginal producing location m establishes the market price, since it would have both zero profits and zero rental value of land in a competitive economy. Thus, we can define the market price in j as equal to the average variable cost plus transport cost in the marginal region m:

$$P_i^j = \text{AVC}_i^m + T_i^{mj} \quad \begin{matrix} i = 1, \ldots, N \\ j = 1, \ldots, M. \end{matrix} \quad (9.2)$$

By substituting equation (9.2) into equation (9.1) we obtain:

$$\text{LR}_i^k = (\text{AVC}_i^m - \text{AVC}_i^k) + (T_i^{mj} - T_i^{kj}) \quad \begin{matrix} i = 1, \ldots, N \\ j,k = 1, \ldots, M; \end{matrix} \quad (9.3)$$

which shows that the locational rent is equal to the difference between the average variable costs at the marginal location and location k, plus the difference between transport costs.

Note from equation (9.1) that the location rent is a gross concept which can take the form of either profits or rental value of land. At any producing location, the producer pays the landlord the rental value of the land; and the difference between that and the location rent is profit.[1] *At any given time, if some producing locations have positive profits, there will be incentives for change.* Landlords will increase rents, and firms will relocate. We are concerned with both adjustments, but the primary focus will be on the change in locations.

Now let us examine what would happen if firms were to move to more favorable locations. The supply curves in all markets would shift — some up, some down. The increased production at the favorable locations would create additional demand for labor and an increase in the wage rates. The labor force would relocate in response to higher wage rates and excess demand at the favorable locations. However, the process is not finished. If labor were to move to the favorable producing locations, the demand for goods at these locations would increase, changing prices at all locations. Since commodities are inputs as well as outputs, the price of commodity inputs would change. The movement of firms in industry i would have an effect on the prices that are paid by other industries that use commodity i, and would in turn have a feedback on the price of inputs used by industry i.

We can conclude that if there is a movement of output to more favorable locations in any one industry, the price of all commodities and inputs will change, causing location rents and profits to change for all industries in all locations. There is no way theoretically to determine the magnitude or direction of these changes. Both the supply and demand curves for all commodities and inputs shift; some changes cause shifts in one direction, and other changes cause shifts in another direction.

These locational changes can be viewed as a recursive process. At the beginning of any period there is a set of prices, and thus profits. Industries relocate during the period in response to these profits. The relocations cause changes in all prices, and additional relocations occur in the next period.

The next section describes the formulation of this theoretical framework into an econometric model.

9.4 THE MODEL

The principal driving force in the model is a set of industry location equations that explain the change in output by region. The explanatory variables in the model, as published in Harris (1973), include the marginal transportation cost of shipping goods out of each region, the marginal transportation costs of obtaining inputs at the place of production, the cost of labor, the value of land, prior investments, prior production, and agglomeration variables which are identified as population density, major buyers, and major suppliers.

The agglomeration variables represent external effects on the industry. In addition to transportation costs, and other costs listed in the equation, the proximity of buyers or suppliers and population density may cause external economies or diseconomies to the industry. Population density may represent an availability of trained labor supply which would reduce the cost of training. On the other hand, to firms in other industries, high density may mean congestion and external diseconomies. The proximity of buyers and suppliers may represent external economies that do not show up in transportation rates, such as the reduction in the time lost in the transfer of goods and improved communications among firms by allowing managers to have face-to-face contact.

The transportation variables used in the equations need further explanation. An industry in a given location may sell its goods to many different markets, or may buy its materials from different locations; but what is needed are transport rates that reflect the shipment of the marginal units of output and input. These shadow prices are derived from a linear programming algorithm, and are used as transportation variables in the model. The transportation linear programming algorithm is run for each of the industries that produce commodities. For example, in explaining the location of the steel industry, we use the marginal transportation cost of shipping steel to the markets from the place of production; and we also use the marginal transportation cost of obtaining coal, iron ore, or other inputs into the regions with steel production.

One of the most important determinants of changes in output is the existence of capital stock. Once a plant has located, it is likely to produce at that location for some time. The location may have been a good one when the plant was originally built; however, in the meantime, because of the changing location of markets and suppliers, the existing location may no longer be a good one. The abandonment of an existing plant does not occur rapidly; decreases in output occur slowly over time in line with the depreciation of the old plant. Once profits at a new location are high enough to pay the remaining fixed costs of the old location, the old plant will be abandoned. We do not have data on the age or value of capital stock by region; therefore, as substitutes in the equations, we use the level of output and prior equipment purchases. Equipment purchases represent gross, not net, investment, and output represents depreciation. There is a problem, however, in that the output variable is also an agglomeration variable. That is, for some location decisions it would be an indication of the amount of competition that exists in each location, and high levels of output could discourage location of new capacity. On the other hand, in other industries the high level of output may encourage new capacity, since firms may share the same labor pool.

Since the book (Harris, 1973) has been published, there have been a few modifications in the industry location equations. The marginal transportation cost of shipping products, the marginal transportation costs of obtaining inputs, and the labor costs have all been converted to location rents and combined into a single variable.[2] Instead of having separate variables for a few major buyers in each industry, total demand is included as one variable. Instead of separate variables for a few major suppliers, one variable measuring input scarcity is used, which is a measure of the amount of inputs that have be imported into the region per dollar of output. Changing the equations served two purposes: by reducing the number of variables, the problems of multicollinearity were reduced; and by converting the cost variables into location rents, it is possible to expand the types of applications of the model. For example, if we wish to evaluate the effects of pollution control regulations for industries in Maryland, we can adjust the location rents by additional treatment costs.

Once output by industry is determined, then related variables such as investment, employment, and earnings are estimated. We forecast equipment purchases by industry, and construction expenditures by the type of construction — including seventeen types of private construction and eleven types of public construction. The decision to locate industry output and investment is one and the same. If the production decision calls for increases in output, it may also call for increases in capital stock. Therefore, industrial investment is related to the changes in output and the level of output.

The other major behavioral relationships in the model are the location decisions by individuals. We have equations to explain population migration by age-race group, with the explanatory variables being wage rates, changes in employment, and the amount of labor surplus or deficit. If an area's unemployment rate is higher than the national unemployment rate, there is a labor surplus; if it is lower, there is a labor deficit. Forecasts of births and deaths are added to population to obtain the population forecasts.

Once population has been located, then related variables such as personal income by residence and personal consumption expenditures are forecast. The model also forecasts foreign exports and imports located by the ports of entry or departure. Total demand by industry sector is then derived. It consists of intermediate demand, which is obtained by applying technical input-output coefficients to the regional outputs, and final demand, which consists of personal consumption expenditures, government expenditures by eight functional categories, construction expenditures by twenty-eight types, equipment purchases by sixty-nine sectors, and foreign exports. The personal consumer expenditures, the defense expenditures, and foreign exports are forecast by industry sector. The industry composition of the investment expenditures is derived by applying capital coefficients to the totals. The total supply of goods in an area is derived by adding the regional output and foreign imports together.

The model is recursive. The change in industry output is forecast by values that exist at the beginning of the period or from historical periods. Then all other variables are derived for the forecast year. As a result, the values of all of the explanatory variables in the output equations change. These new values are used to forecast output in the next year. The model is diagrammed in figure 9–1.

The regional forecasts are controlled to the national forecast produced by Clopper Almon's Interindustry Forecasting Model (INFORUM) (1974).

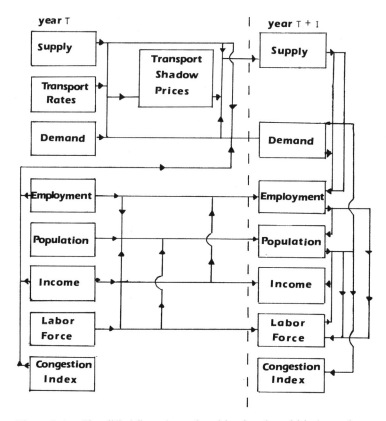

Figure 9–1.   Simplified flow chart of multiregional, multi-industry forecasting model

Source: Harris, Curtis C., Jr. *The Urban Economies, 1985: A Multiregional, Multi-Industry Forecasting Model,* (Lexington, Mass.: D.C. Heath and Company, 1973).

All the equations in the regional model were fitted on a shares basis. Therefore, the model forecasts each region's share of a national number, and the regional value is determined by multiplying the share by that national number. The tie-in with the national model not only assures a reasonable set of forecasts, but it also expands the range of applications of the model. In certain applications we proceed by first making exogenous changes in the national model, then in the regional model. For example, forecasts of prices are done in the national model; therefore, we find the effect of price changes on national industry outputs before finding the effect on the regional economies.

9.5 APPLICATIONS

Impacts of alternative government decisions are evaluated by making two runs of the forecasting model. The first run is made under normal assumptions, which treats every variable in some endogenous way. Either the variables are forecast with functional relationships, or, as in the case of defense expenditures, it is assumed that the regional distribution will remain constant. The second run of the model makes exogenous changes in one or more variables. For example, the impact under study could be an exogenous change in the regional distribution of defense expenditures, the location of highway construction, or the location of a major industry. Comparison of the numbers from the two runs gives impact measures of the changes. The model is constructed so that the impact measures are not strongly influenced by the forecast levels. That is, it would be possible to have a bad forecast with the normal run of the model, but reasonable measures of impact.

9.5.1 Transportation Applications

One of the major applications of the model has been in evaluating alternative highways. A major study was done for the Federal Highway Administration (Harris, 1974) to evaluate alternative highway systems. Five alternative highway systems were evaluated:

1. the base year system assumed that no new national highways would be built after the base year;
2. the completed interstate system assumed the interstate would be completed as scheduled;
3. the extended primary system assumed that the interstate system would be extended to smaller cities;
4. the economic development system assumed that the interstate system would be extended to the poorest areas of the country; and
5. the urban system assumed that urban area highways would be built in order to reduce traffic congestion.

A given dollar amount of total national highway construction was assumed to be available, and each alternative specified which regions would have segments of the national highway system. All highways in the national systems would be of interstate quality, and funds not used for a national system were allocated to regions in the normal endogenous way.

The transportation rates that were used in the linear programming algorithms were estimated using ICC formulas, and allowed for competition between rail and truck shipments. The formulas were applied by weight category to each commodity. For a given weight class and a given origin and destination both the cost of shipping by truck and the cost of shipping by rail were computed, and the lower of the two was selected. This was done for all weight classes, approximately ten for each commodity, and then an average transportation rate was estimated using the distribution of shipments by weight class. Thus, a transportation rate between any two regions could be a composite of both rail and truck shipments, or it could be all truck or all rail shipments. Shipments in the low weight classes and over long distances could go by rail.

The ICC formulas consist of three parts: (1) the terminal cost at the origin; (2) the terminal cost at the destination; and (3) the line-haul cost between the regions. The terminal costs are broadly defined to include all pick-up and delivery costs, and thus can be thought of as intra-area costs. We would expect a new highway system to have an effect on the line-haul costs of shipping by truck. We estimated this change using DOT's national highway transportation network model, which computes the minimum time path between each pair of regions. The travel time between regions was changed to the cost of operating trucks, and when we ran the model it produced the path that would minimize the cost of operating trucks between areas. DOT had coded the network model for the base year under the assumption that the interstate highway system was completed. We made additional changes in the network for the new highway system examined in this study. By running DOT's network model in the base year, and for one of the alternative systems, we found the line-haul cost savings associated with operating trucks between each pair of regions. We then changed this line-haul cost in the ICC formulas and reran the linear programming algorithms with the new lower truck rates. This produced a shift from rail to truck shipment, and changed the marginal transportation costs associated with shipping goods in and out of each region.

We also introduced a highway congestion variable into the model, which was defined as the vehicle miles traveled divided by the capacity miles of service. The highway congestion variable was used to help explain industry location. Vehicle miles traveled was related to population and the construction capacity miles of service was related to highway construction, thus allowing the congestion index to change over time.

In the model, the construction of a new highway system has an immediate impact on regional economies, with multiplying effects during the construction phase. In the long run the economies are affected by changes in the transportation rates and the congestion index.

We also evaluated the energy-saving effects of piggyback shipments. We introduced the ICC formulas for piggyback shipments and recomputed the transportation rates between areas, assuming that all truck shipments greater than one hundred miles would go by piggyback. The results of this study indicated that savings were small, since most of the truck fuel consumption takes place on short trips and for pick-up and delivery within a metropolitan area.

The results of these applications have been published elsewhere, and therefore will not be reported here. One point to note is that the magnitude of impacts varied widely from region to region. There is no such thing as a one-regional multiplier that could be applied to highway construction in all regions. For a given dollar investment, some regions had large changes, others had small changes. The alternative runs show a redistribution of economic activity, and the economic development system, for example, would help the poorest areas in the nation by stimulating their growth and increasing their capital income. Gains in any one region, however, were always offset by losses elsewhere, since it was assumed that the total amount of the national highway expenditures would be the same in each alternative.

We have also used the model to evaluate small segments of the interstate highways. One of these was the construction of I-84 in the four-county area between Hartford, Connecticut, and Providence, Rhode Island (Harris, 1976). The segment is considered in isolation from the national network; therefore, we allowed the intra-area cost to change as opposed to the line-haul costs. It was estimated exogenously that the truck costs on the new highway would be 14 percent less than the cost on the existing route between Hartford and Providence, but that this route only accounts for 10 percent of the total freight shipments in the area. The results of this application are summarized in table 9-1. The highway was to be constructed between 1979

Table 9-1.   Impact of Interstate Highway 84 between Hartford, Conn. and Providence, R.I.*

Year	Normal forecasts		Exogenous changes		Total changes	
	GRP	Jobs	Investment	Jobs	GRP	Jobs
1979	14,093,889	1,030,302	48,300	1189	27,045	1697
1980	14,927,805	1,072,456	34,000	894	25,051	1664
1981	15,705,738	1,111,351	44,200	1140	29,847	1936
1982	16,513,098	1,149,011	20,100	559	17,272	1176
1983	17,402,991	1,188,775	10,600	295	10,094	680
1984	18,310,386	1,230,809			2,707	202
1985	19,291,433	1,274,916			1,844	118
1990	24,615,812	1,501,599			1,555	91

*Assumes intra-area transportation rates decline 1.4 percent starting in 1983.

Data are for four counties—Hartford, Conn.; Tolland, Conn.; Windham, Conn.; and Providence, R.I. All dollar figures are in thousands using 1972 prices.

and 1983, with the reduction in transportation costs starting in 1983. Note in the table that the ratio of changes in Gross Regional Product (GRP) to highway investment is less than 1 during the construction, but that it approaches 1 by 1983. This is explained by the role of imports into the four-county area, and because the income multiplying effect of the investment is spread over several years. In order to undertake this highway construction it was necessary that a large proportion of the highway money be spent for goods and materials produced in other regions, but, over time, the added demand for materials in the four-county area stimulates local industry. By 1990 most of the dynamic relationship had a chance to work out, and the increase in Gross Regional Product over the normal run can be considered a longrun impact of the highway construction. I would expect that this approximate level of Gross Regional Product would be maintained in the years beyond 1990.

In comparing the increment to construction jobs with the total change in jobs, the more normal multiplier effect is noticeable. That is, there are more total jobs created than construction jobs, and by 1983 the ratio is greater than two. By 1990 there is an increase of 91 jobs over the normal forecast. This longrun effect seems rather minor, and has stirred a lot of controversy in Connecticut. The prohighway people did not like the results because it showed that there are not high longrun benefits from highway construction. The antihighway people did not like it because they had previously argued against the highway on the grounds that there would be too much pollution associated with the growth caused by the highway.

There are several reasons why this small longrun impact occurred. One is the nature of the highway under study. The highway would account for only about 10 percent of the total freight shipments in the area, and the decrease of 1.4 percent in the intra-area transportation cost was small. The other reasons have to do with changes that occur in other variables in the model, and will be explained shortly after the next example.

Table 9-2 shows the results of transportation investment in Pitt County, North Carolina (*Transportation . . .*, 1976). Transportation investment included the construction of Interstate Highway 264 and the upgrading of all railroads in the county. Note the negative signs in the changes in Gross Regional Product and jobs after the construction period. These results seem typical of those that occured in the 1950s and 1960s throughout the Midwest, when a number of ghost towns were created and many small towns lost population. There were two reasons generally given for these changes: the decline in the number of farmers, brought about by increased productivity in agriculture; and the building of major high-speed highways, which allowed the farmers and their families to travel greater distances to larger

Table 9-2.   Impact of transportation investment in Pitt County, North Carolina*

Year	Normal forecasts		Exogenous changes		Total changes	
	GRP	Jobs	Investment	Jobs	GRP	Jobs
1976	382,208	31,006	33,412	918	17,817	1,258
1977	402,981	31,798	29,546	785	16,651	1,125
1978	421,081	32,428			1,131	136
1981	470,371	33,862			− 367	6
1984	518,896	35,034			− 1,000	− 38
1987	568,343	36,227			− 1,061	− 40
1990	619,523	37,407			− 1,114	− 40

*Construction of Interstate Highway 264 in Pitt County and the upgrading of all railroads in County. It is estimated that there would be a 22 percent decline in intra-area truck rates affecting 39 percent of the truck shipments, and a 9 percent reduction in intra-area rail rates affecting 100 percent of the rail shipments, starting in 1978.

All dollar figures are in thousands using 1972 prices.

urban areas to do their shopping for farm and household supplies. The results of applying this model to Pitt County indicate that highway improvement itself can explain declines in an area.

In the context of the model, this longrun decline in Pitt County and the small increase in Connecticut and Rhode Island can be explained by the effect highway construction has on other variables in the model. A reduction in transportation rates works both ways in its effects on industry location. If an industry is already located in an area and transportation costs are reduced, there will be a greater incentive for the industry to stay in its present location, and less incentive for the industry to move to areas with previously lower transportation costs. However, if an industry is importing inputs from other regions with high transportation costs, the lower transportation costs would reduce the incentive of the supplier to move to the area that is demanding the supplies. Suppliers would have a tendency to remain where they are. Thus, lowering transportation costs can increase output in some industries and decrease output in others.

The value of land and input scarcity variables are also affected by the transportation construction. During the construction phase the value of land increases, and thus discourages the location of industry. Also, since there is a large increase in demand for goods to be used in construction, the input scarcity variable increases. Since inputs have to be used for construction, there are fewer available for other uses, which discourages increases in industry output. The increase in demand also has an endogenous effect on the marginal transportation costs. It increases the cost of moving goods into the county, and decreases the cost of shipping goods that are already being produced in the county. The net balance of this effect could be negative.

In Pitt County the transportation investment was large relative to the Gross Regional Product; therefore, the increase in demand created by construction had substantial impacts on the other variables. In the Hartford-Providence case, the highway construction was only a small part of the Gross Regional Product; therefore, the adverse impacts caused by the increases in demand were not as severe.

If growth in Pitt County is not helped by highway construction, would it be helped by zeroing out all transportation investment? The answer is no. Table 9-3 shows the result when all transportation investments are set to zero. In every year total change in Gross Regional Product and jobs is negative. In this application, transportation rates were allowed to increase in relation to the increase in population. If population were to increase rapidly, highway congestion would increase, and this would have an effect on the transportation rates of Pitt County relative to the other counties in the nation. However, population growth in the area was not very rapid; therefore, there was not much loss due to increase of transportation rates. Also, the decrease in total demand for goods was not very much, and this minimized a secondary effect on other variables.

Table 9-3.   Impact of zero transportation investment in Pitt County, North Carolina*

Year	Normal forecasts		Exogenous changes		Total changes	
	GRP	Jobs	Investment	Jobs	GRP	Jobs
1976	382,208	31,006	−2174	−63	−1232	−87
1977	402,981	31,798	−2168	−63	−1412	−99
1978	421,081	32,428	−2137	−62	−1428	−99
1981	470,371	33,862	−2103	−61	−1339	−93
1984	518,896	35,034	−2080	−60	−1314	−91
1987	568,343	36,227	−2056	−59	−1199	−82
1990	619,523	37,407	−2034	−59	−1174	−78

*Assumes that transportation rates increase the same percentage as population.
All dollar figures in thousands using 1972 prices.

9.5.2 Offshore Oil Applications

Another major application of the model has been to study the onshore impacts of offshore oil and gas development. So far about thirty runs of the model have been made for different scenarios specifying offshore oil development in various sections of the country. Our first study was for the New England area, for which nine alternative runs were made (Grigalunas, 1975). These runs specified the price of oil and gas, the level of oil find, whether or not refineries would be built onshore, and whether or not the state or federal government would control the royalties.

Since these runs, the Supreme Court has ruled that the federal government will receive the royalties, but the results of the runs show that the major impacts on the New England area would occur if the states received the royalties. The additional state revenue from the royalties would have increased government expenditures and decreased taxes, thereby increasing disposable income and personal consumer expenditures. When the federal government receives the money, only a small part comes back to the New England region.

Other runs have been made for the mid-Atlantic and South Atlantic regions, but only the results of an application for the mid-Atlantic region will be reported. These results were the basis for the economic impact study by the Bureau of Land Management on the Baltimore Canyon Lease-Sale (Reinfeld and Collahan, n.d.). The key assumptions for the mid-Atlantic application were:

1. The price of oil was set at $11 per barrel and the price of gas at $1 per thousand cubic feet.
2. It was assumed that present harbor facilities were adequate to service offshore oil wells.
3. Exploratory drilling is to start in 1976 and production of oil in 1980.
4. Investments reach a peak in 1983 and production reaches a peak in 1990; the oil is assumed to be exhausted by year 2000; at peak production there are to be forty-four platforms with twenty wells each, each well producing 850 barrels per day.
5. Pipeline land terminals and gas processing plants were to be built in four New Jersey coastal counties — Atlantic, Manmouth, Cape May, and Ocean.
6. Oil was to be piped overland from these terminals to refineries in the Philadelphia-Delware area and upper New Jersey-New York areas.
7. It was assumed that foreign imports of oil could be reduced by the amount of oil production in the mid-Atlantic; therefore, no new oil refinery capacity would be needed.

For the operation of the model we specified the investment in exploratory wells, development wells, platforms, pipelines, terminals, gas processing plants, and pollution equipment. Any investment in offshore facilities was assigned to the county that would service the facilities. We also specified the amount of gas and oil output and the amount of employment, both for oil and gas production and for construction. To operate the model we could have set either the level of investment or the level of output, and the model would have generated the other number and the employment. We set the investment, output, and employment separately, since it was found that both the capital requirements and the employment requirements were different for offshore drilling than they were for onshore drilling.

The whole region consisted of eighty-one counties, and the impact on the complete region was less than 1 percent. The initial impact occurred in industrial activity, then spread to services in other years. It occurred initially in the coastal counties, and with time spread to the other counties. In New Jersey there was induced activity in construction, trade, transportation, machines, and manufacturing in metals. Production from capital intensive industries was still imported into New Jersey. During the major construction period people migrated into the area, but then migrated back out again as construction slowed down. The two counties most affected were Cape May and Atlantic. Table 9–4 shows the results for Atlantic County. The investment numbers and employment numbers for exogenous changes were only those associated for Atlantic County, and not the entire Atlantic region. As a result of the oil development, Gross Regional Product in Atlantic County in 1990 was 23 percent higher than under the normal forecast. Al-

Table 9–4.   Impact of offshore oil and gas development in Atlantic County, N.J.

Year	Normal forecasts GRP	Normal forecasts Jobs	Exogenous changes Investment	Exogenous changes Jobs const.	Exogenous changes Jobs industry	Total changes GRP	Total changes Jobs
1978	NA	NA	17,518			NA	NA
1979	NA	NA	54,476	332		NA	NA
1980	1,065,874	79,250	239,330	397	202	90,641	5081
1981	NA	NA	98,462	446	230	NA	NA
1982	NA	NA	121,646	438	246	NA	NA
1983	NA	NA	124,501	470	270	NA	NA
1984	NA	NA	84,512	470	294	NA	NA
1985	1,202,515	83,511	131,253	470	357	253,037	2368
1986	NA	NA	81,657	463	373	NA	NA
1987	NA	NA	48,441	338	385	NA	NA
1988	NA	NA	63,104	289	397	NA	NA
1989	NA	NA	44,635	289	409	NA	NA
1990	1,377,827	89,818	19,505	208	417	412,667	1545

NA = number not printed during computer runs.
All dollar figures in thousands using 1972 prices.

though we did not print out results for every year, the results given in the table show that Gross Regional Product continued to grow throughout the period. However, the employment increases reached a peak during the major construction phase and then declined, since construction is labor-intensive and oil production is not. Although investment in any one year can have impacts over a number of years, the results show that the initial investment did not increase Gross Regional Product nearly as much as the amount of investment. Not only is the investment impact spread out over a number of years, but over time industries responded to the oil production activity. Industry output slowly built up in Atlantic County, replacing supply that was previously imported from other parts of the nation.

9.5.3 Other Applications

The model has also been used to study the effects of public employment programs (National Planning Association, 1974); the impact of reduced agriculture production in the southwestern United States (Bender, et al., 1976); and the impact of natural gas cutbacks on the Maryland economy (Donnelly and Parhizgari, 1975). The model is presently being used to study the impact of the automobile industry on the Detroit area (Southwest Michigan Council of Governments, n.d.).

9.6 CONCLUSION

The Multiregional, Multi-Industry Forecasting Model has proven to be very useful. A reasonable set of forecasts is produced under normal assumptions, and tests of the model's accuracy have been good. Using only 1965 and 1966 data, the model predicted certain changes of trends that have become apparent in the 1970s, such as the relative increase in growth in the South and the slowdown of growth in the far West. The model also produced reasonable measurements of impact of exogenous changes. If exogenous investment is maintained over the years, the model shows multiplier effects on the regional economies that are similar to those produced with static models; but unlike the static models, the MRMI model shows that the multiplier effect stops when the investment stops, and that under certain conditions investment can have negative effects on an economy.

Even though the model is useful now, we are not content. A major effort is underway to collect recent data on an annual basis. With this data we will be able to pool time-series and cross-section data to obtain more reliable estimates of the parameters. The data will allow us to incorporate more appropriate time lags into the location equations, and, furthermore, to estimate a *unique constant* for each region by industry. This unique constant would measure the region's attractiveness vis-a-vis other regions.

Notes

1. Dunn (1954) has shown that with completely competitive land markets the landlord would receive the entire location rent.
2. Equation (9.3) shows that location rent can be broken down into that associated with average variable costs, and that associated with transport cost. If the various components of average variable cost were specified, such as labor and materials, then additional components of location rent would be derived. When suppliers sell to more than one market, location rents can be estimated with linear programming — see Stevens (1961).

BIBLIOGRAPHY

Advisory Commission on Intergovernmental Relations, *Significant Features of Fiscal Federalism 1976-77 Edition, 3. Expenditures,* Washington, D.C.: U.S. Government Printing Office (1977).

Almon, C., Jr., *The American Economy to 1975,* New York: Harper and Row (1966).

Almon, C., Jr., et al., *1985: Interindustry Forecasts of the American Economy,* Lexington, Mass.: Lexington Books (1974).

Anderson, R. J., Jr., "A Note on Economic Base Studies and Regional Econometric Forecasting Models," *Journal of Regional Science* 10:325-333 (1970).

Barro, R. and H. Grossman, "A General Disequilibrium Model of Income and Employment," *American Economic Review* 61:82-93 (1971).

Barro, R. and H. Grossman, *Money, Employment and Inflation,* New York: Cambridge University Press (1976).

Bell, F. W., "An Econometric Forecasting Model for a Region," *Journal of Regional Science* 7:109-127 (1967).

Bender, F., et al., *Solar Energy Applications in Agriculture: Potential, Research Needs and Adoption Strategies,* Report to Agriculture Resource Service, U.S. Department of Agriculture (1976).

Barnard, J. R. and W. T. Dent, "Regional Econometric Models and State Tax Revenue Forecasts: The Case for Iowa," paper presented to the Midcontinent Regional Science Association (1977).

Billings, R., "The Mathematical Identity of the Multipliers Derived from the Economic Base Model and the Input-Output Model," *Journal of Regional Science* 9:471–473 (1969).

Black, S. W. and H. H. Kelejian, "A Macro Model of the U.S. Labor Market," *Econometrica* 38:712–741 (1970).

Blanco, C., "The Determinants of Interstate Population Movements," *Journal of Regional Science* 5:77–84 (1963).

Blanco, C., "Prospective Unemployment and Interstate Population Movements," *Review of Economics and Statistics* 46:221–222 (1964).

Bourque, P., et al., *The Washington Economy: An Input-Output Study.* Seattle: Graduate School of Business Administration and the Department of Commerce and Economic Development, University of Washington (1967).

Bourque, P. J., "An Input-Output Analysis of Economic Change in Washington State," *University of Washington Business Review* 30:5–22 (1971a).

Bourque, P., *An Input-Output Analysis of Economic Change in Washington State,* Seattle: Graduate School of Business Administration, University of Washington (1971b).

Bradley, I. E. and J. P. Gander, "Input-Output Multipliers: Some Theoretical Comments," *Journal of Regional Science* 9:309–317 (1969).

Brodsky, H. and D. E. Sarfaty. "Measuring the Economic Base in a Developing Country," *Land Economics* 53:445–454 (1977).

Bureau of Labor Statistics, "The 1972-73 Consumer Expenditure Survey," U.S. Department of Labor (n.d.).

Chalmers, J. et al., "Spatial Interaction in Sparsely Populated Regions: an Hierarchical Economic Base Approach," *International Regional Science Review* 3:75–92 (1978).

Chenery, H., "Regional Analysis," in H. Chenery and P. Clark (eds.), *The Structure and Growth of the Italian Economy,* Rome: U.S. Mutual Security Agency (1953).

Chen, D., "A Tabular Survey of Selected Regional Econometric Models," Working Paper No. 11, San Francisco: Federal Reserve Bank of San Francisco (1972).

Clark, D. H. and J. D. Coupe, *The Bangor Area Economy: Its Present and Future.* Bangor, Maine: College of Business Administration, University of Maine (1967).

Clower, R. W., "The Keynesian Counterrevolution: A Theoretical Appraisal," in F. Hahn and F. Brechling (eds.), *The Theory of Interest Rates,* London: Macmillan (1965).

Coughlin, R. E., et al., *The Economic Impact on Ports of Philadelphia Commerce,* Regional Science Research Institute Report No. 52 (1977).

Crow, R. T., "A Nationally Linked Regional Econometric Model," *Journal of Regional Science* 13:187–204 (1973).

Czamanski, S., and E. Malizia, "Applicability and Limitations in the Use of National Input-Output Tables for Regional Studies," *Papers of the Regional Science Association* 23:65–77 (1969).

Doeksen, G. A. and C. H. Little, "Effects of Size of the Input-Output Model on the Results of an Impact Analysis," *Agricultural Economics Research* 20:134–138 (1968).

Donnelly, W. and A. Parhizgari, "Estimating the Regional Impact of Energy Shortages," paper presented at the International Regional Science Conference on Energy and Environment, Louvain, Belgium (1975).

Dunn, E. S., *The Location of Agricultural Production,* Gainesville, Fla.: University of Florida Press (1954).

Dutta, M., and V. Su, *An Econometric Model of Puerto Rico,* mimeo (1969).

Engle, R., "Issues in the Specification of an Econometric Model of Metropolitan Growth," *Journal of Urban Economics* 1:250-267 (1974).

Engle, R. et al., "An Econometric Simulation Model of Intra-Metropolitan Housing Location: Housing, Business, Transportation, and Local Government," *American Economic Review Papers and Proceedings* 62:87-98 (1972).

Evans, M. K., *Macroeconomic Activity,* New York: Harper and Row (1969).

Fair, R. C., *The Short-Run Demand for Workers and Hours,* Amsterdam: North-Holland (1969).

Fair, R. C., *A Model of Macroeconomic Activity,* 2v. Cambridge, Mass.: Ballinger (1974, 1976).

(Jack) Faucett Associates, Inc., *Employment Effects of the Final System Plan,* prepared for the U.S. Railway Association, Chevy Chase, Maryland: Jack Faucett Associates, Inc., (1975).

Fei, J. C., "A Fundamental Theorem for the Aggregation Problem of Input-Output Analysis," *Econometrica* 24:400-412 (1956).

Field, R. and F. Convery, "Estimating Local Economic Impacts in Land-Use Planning," *Journal of Forestry* 74:155-156 (1976).

Fishkind, H., "The Regional Impact of Monetary Policy: An Econometric Simulation Study of Indiana, 1958-1973," *Journal of Regional Science* 17:77-88 (1977).

Gamble, H. B. and D. L. Raphael, *A Microregional Analysis of Clinton County, Pennsylvania.* University Park, Pennsylvania: The Pennsylvania Regional Analysis Group, The Pennsylvania State University (1965).

Garnick, D. H. "Disaggregated Basic-Service Models and Regional Input-Output Models in Multiregional Projections," *Journal of Regional Science* 9:87-100 (1969).

Garnick, D. H., "Differential Regional Multiplier Models," *Journal of Regional Science* 10:35-47 (1970).

Gerking, S., "Some Statistical Problems in Estimating Stochastic Input-Output Models." Unpublished Ph.D. dissertation, Indiana University (1975).

Gerking, S., "Input-Output as a Simple Econometric Model,"*Review of Economics and Statistics* 58:274-282 (1976).

Gerking, S. and S. Pleeter, "Minimum Variance Sampling and Input-Output Analysis," *Review of Regional Studies* 7:59-80 (1978).

Glickman, N. J., "An Econometric Model for the Philadelphia Region," *Journal of Regional Science* 11:15-32 (1971).

Glickman, N. J., "Son of the Specification of Regional Econometric Models," *Papers of the Regional Science Association* 32:155-177 (1974).

Glickman, N. J., *Econometric Analysis of Regional Systems: Explorations in Model Building and Policy Analysis,* New York: Academic (1977).

Goldberger, A. S., *Impact Multipliers and Dynamic Properties of the Klein-Goldberger Model,* Amsterdam: North-Holland (1959).

Golladay, L. and R. H. Haveman, *The Economic Impacts of Tax-Transfer Policy: Regional and Distributional Effects,* New York: Academic (1977).

Greytak, D., "A Statistical Analysis of Regional Export Estimating Techniques," *Journal of Regional Science* 9:387–395 (1969).

Greytak, D., "Regional Consumption Patterns and the Heckscher-Ohlin Trade Theorem," *Journal of Regional Science* 15:39–45 (1975).

Grigalunas, T., *Offshore Petroleum and New England,* Marine Technical Report No. 39, Kingston, R. I.: University of Rhode Island (1975).

Grubb, H. W., *The Structure of the Texas Economy,* Austin, Tex.: Office of Information Services, Office of the Governor (1973).

Haig, R., "Toward an Understanding of the Metropolis: Some Speculations Regarding the Economic Basis of Urban Concentration," *Quarterly Journal of Economics* 40:179–208 (1926).

Harris, C. C., Jr., *The Urban Economies, 1985: A Multiregional, Multi-Industry Forecasting Model,* Lexington, Mass.: Lexington Books (1973).

Harris, C. C., Jr., *Regional Economic Effects of Alternative Highway Systems,* Cambridge, Mass.: Ballinger Publishing Co. (1974).

Harris, C. C., Jr., "Report on the Impact of Interstate 84 Between Providence and Hartford." Prepared for Close, Jensen and Miller, Wethersfield, Connecticut (1976).

Hay, G. A., "Production, Price and Inventory Theory," *American Economic Review* 60:531–545 (1970).

Heilbrun, J., *Urban Economics and Public Policy,* New York: St. Martin's Press (1974).

Hewings, G. J. D., "Input-Output Models: Aggregation for Regional Impact Analysis," *Growth and Change* 3:15–19 (1972).

Hildebrand, G. and A. Mace, Jr., "The Employment Multiplier in an Expanding Industrial Market: Los Angeles County, 1940–47," *Review of Economics and Statistics* 32:241–249 (1950).

Hill, E., "Calculation of Trade Flows and Income Multipliers Using the Multiregional Input-Output Model," MRIO Working Paper No. 3, prepared for the University Research Program, U.S. Department of Transportation (1975).

Hirsch, W. Z., *Urban Economic Analysis,* New York: McGraw-Hill (1973).

Hirsch, W. Z., "Interindustry Relations of a Metropolitan Area," *Review of Economics and Statistics* 41:360–369 (1959).

Hotelling, H., "Stability in Competition," *Economic Journal* 39:41–57 (1929).

Hoyt, H., "A Method for Measuring the Value of Imports into an Urban Community," *Land Economics* 37:150–161 (1961).

Isard, W., "Regional Commodity Balances and Interregional Commodity Flows," *American Economic Review Papers and Proceedings* 43:167–180 (1953a).

Isard, W., *Location and Space-Economy,* Cambridge, Mass.: MIT Press (1956).

Isard, W., *Methods of Regional Analysis: An Introduction to Regional Science,* Englewood Cliffs, N.J.: Prentice-Hall, Inc. (1960).

Isard, W., and T. W. Langford, Jr., "Impact of Vietnam War Expenditures on the Philadelphia Economy: Some Initial Experiments with the Inverse of the Philadelphia Input-Output Table," *Papers of the Regional Science Association* 23:217–265 (1969).

Isard, W. and T. W. Langford, Jr., *Regional Input-Output Study: Recollections Reflections, and Diverse Notes on the Philadelphia Experience,* Cambridge, Mass.: MIT Press (1971).

Isard, W., T. W. Langford, and E. Romanoff, *The Philadelphia Region Input-Output Study,* Philadelphia: Regional Science Research Institute, mimeo (1967).

Isserman, A. M., "Regional Employment Multiplier: A New Approach; Comment," *Land Economics* 51:290–293 (1975).

Isserman, A. M., "The Location Quotient Approach to Estimating Regional Economic Impacts," *Journal of the American Institute of Planners* 43:33–41 (1977a).

Isserman, A. M., "A Bracketing Approach for Estimating Regional Economic Impact Multipliers and a Procedure for Assessing Their Accuracy," *Environment and Planning* 9:1003–1011 (1977b).

Isserman, A. M., "Design of a County-level, Industry-specific Employment Data Base," Planning Paper, Bureau of Planning Research, University of Illinois at Urbana-Champaign (1977c).

Kendrick, J. W. and C. Jaycox, "The Concept and Estimation of Gross State Product," *The Southern Economic Journal* 32:153–168 (1965).

Kim, U., C. Park, and S. Kwak, "An Application of the Interregional I/O Model for the study of the Impact of the McClellan-Kerr Arkansas River Multiple Purpose Project," prepared for the Institute for Water Resources, U.S. Army Corps of Engineers (1975).

Klein, L. R. and N. J. Glickman, "Econometric Model Building at Regional Level," *Regional Science and Urban Economics* 7:3–23 (1977).

Langford, T. and R. E. Coughlin, *Report on the Baltimore Region Input-Output Study,* Regional Science Research Institute Report No. 23 (1971).

Lefeber, L., *Allocation in Space,* Amsterdam: North-Holland (1958).

Leigh, R., "The Use of Location Quotients in Urban Economic Base Studies," *Land Economics* 46:202–205 (1972).

Leontief, W. and A. Strout, "Multi-regional Input-Output Analysis," *Proceedings of an International Conference on Input-Output Techniques,* Geneva (1963).

L'Esperance, W. L., *The Structure and Control of a State Economy,* Columbus, Ohio: Ohio State University (1976).

L'Esperance, W. L., G. Nestel, and D. Fromm, "Gross State Product and an Econometric Model of a State," *American Statistical Association Journal* 44:787–807 (1969).

L'Esperance, W. L., A. E. King, and R. H. Sines, "Conjoining an Ohio Input-Output Model with an Econometric Model of Ohio," presented at the 22nd Annual Meetings of the Regional Science Association (1975).

Leven, C. L., "Measuring the Economic Base," *Papers and Proceedings of the Regional Science Association* 2:250–258 (1956).

Lindberg, C. G., "New Mexico's Imports and Exports," *New Mexico Business* (1966).

Malizia, E. and D. L. Bond, "Empirical Tests of the RAS Method of Interindustry Coefficient Adjustment," *Journal of Regional Science* 14:355-365 (1974).

Mathur, V. and H. Rosen, "Regional Employment Multiplier: A New Approach," *Land Economics* 50:93-96 (1974).

Mathur, V. and Rosen, "Regional Employment Multiplier: A New Approach: Reply," *Land Economics* 51:294-295 (1975).

Mattila, J. M., "A Metropolitan Income Determination Model and the Estimation of Metropolitan Income Multipliers," *Journal of Regional Science* 13:1-16 (1973).

Mattila, J. M. and W. R. Thompson, "The Measurement of the Economic Base of a Metropolitan Area," *Land Economics* 31:215-228 (1955).

Mayer, W. and S. Pleeter, "A Theoretical Justification for the Use of Location Quotients," *Regional Science and Urban Economics* (1975).

McCallum, B. T., "Competitive Price Adjustments: An Empirical Study," *American Economic Review* 64:56-65 (1974).

McMenamin, D. G. and J. E. Haring, "An Appraisal of Nonsurvey Techniques for Estimating Regional Input-Output Models," *Journal of Regional Science* 14:101-205 (1974).

McNulty, J. "A Test of the Time Dimension in Economic Base Analysis," *Land Economics* 53:359-368 (1977).

Miernyk, W., *Elements of Input-Output Analysis,* New York: Random House (1965).

Miernyk, W., "Regional and Interregional Input-Output Models: A Reappraisal," in M. Perlman, et al. (eds.), *Spatial, Regional and Population Economics,* New York: Gordon and Breach (1973).

Miernyk, W., "Comments on Recent Developments in Regional Input-Output Analysis," *International Regional Science Review* 1:47-55 (1976).

Miernyk, W., E. Bonner, J. H. Chapman, Jr., and K. Shellhammer, *The Impact of Space and Space-Related Activities on a Local Community: Part I, The Input-Output Analysis,* report submitted to the National Aeronautics and Space Administration (July, 1965).

Miernyk, W., et al., *Simulating Regional Economic Development,* Lexington, Mass.: Lexington Books (1970).

Miller, R. E., "Interregional Feedbacks in Input-Output Models: Some Experimental Results," *Western Economic Journal* 7:41-50 (1969).

Mills, E. S., *Studies in the Structure of the Urban Economy,* Baltimore, Md.: Johns Hopkins Press (1972).

Moore, C., "The Impact of Public Institutions on Regional Income: Upstate Medical Center as a Case in Point," *Economic Geography* 50:124-129 (1974).

Moore, C., "A New Look at the Minimum Requirements Approach to Regional Economic Analysis," *Economic Geography* 51:350-356 (1975).

Moore, F. T., "Regional Economic Reaction Paths," *American Economic Review: Papers and Proceedings* 45:133-148 (1955).

Morre, F. and J. Petersen, "Regional Analysis: An Interindustry Model of Utah," *Review of Economics and Statistics* 37:368-383 (1955).

Morimoto, Y., "On Aggregation Problems in Input-Output Analysis," *Review of Economic Studies* 37:119–126 (1970).

Morrison, W. L. and P. Smith, "Nonsurvey Input-Output Techniques at the Small Area Level: An Evaluation," *Journal of Regional Science* 14:1–14 (1974).

Moses, L. N., "The Stability of Interregional Trading Patterns and Input-Output Analysis," *American Economic Review,* 45:803–832 (1955).

National Planning Association, "An Evaluation of the Economic Impact Project of Public Employment Program," report to the U.S. Department of Labor, Manpower Administration (1974).

Park, S., "Least Squares Estimates of the Regional Employment Multiplier," *Journal of Regional Science* 10:363–374 (1970).

Park, S., "On Input-Output Multipliers with Errors in Input-Output Coefficients," *Journal of Economic Theory* 6:399–403 (1973).

Pfister, R. "On Improving Export Base Studies," *Regional Science Perspectives* 6:105–115 (1976).

Pindyck, R. and D. Rubinfeld, *Econometric Models and Economic Forecasts,* New York: McGraw-Hill (1976).

Polenske, K. R., "The Implementation of a Multiregional Input-Output Model for the United States," in A. Brody and A. P. Carter (eds.), *Input-Output Techniques,* Amsterdam: North-Holland (1972).

Polenske, K., *State Estimates of Technology.* Lexington, Mass.: Lexington Books (1974).

Polenske, K. R., "Multiregional Interactions Between Energy and Transportation," in K. Polenske and J.V. Skolka (eds.), *Advances in Input-Output Analysis,* Cambridge, Mass.: Ballinger Publishing Co. (1976).

Polenske, K. R., "Energy Analysis and the Determination of Multiregional Prices," paper presented at the Twenty-Fifth North American Meetings of the Regional Science Association, Chicago, Illinois, November 11, 1978.

Polenske, K., et al., *State Estimates of the Gross National Product: 1947, 1958, 1963.* Lexington, Mass.: Lexington Books (1972).

Polzin, P. "Urban Employment Models: Estimation and Interpretation," *Land Economics* 59:226–232 (1973).

Polzin, P. "Urban Labor Markets: A Two-Sector Approach," *Growth and Change* 8:11–15 (1977).

Pratt, R. T., "An Appraisal of the Minimum Requirements Technique," *Economic Geography* 44:117–124 (1968).

Preston, R. S., *The Wharton Annual and Industry Forecasting Model,* Studies in Quantitative Economics, No. 7, Philadelphia: Economics Research Unit, University of Pennsylvania (1972).

Pucher, J. R., "Projections of 1980 Freight Demands for Selected Midwestern Railroads," DOT Report No. 14, prepared for the University Research Program, U.S. Department of Transportation (1976).

Quandt, R. E., "Probabilistic Errors in the Leontief System," *Naval Research Logistics Quarterly* 5:155–170 (1958).

Ratajczak, D., "Data Limitations and Alternative Methodology in Estimating Regional Econometric Models," *Review of Regional Studies* 4:51–64 (1974).

Reinfeld, K. and F. Collahan, *Economic Study of the Possible Impacts of a Potential Baltimore Canyon Sale,* Technical Paper No. 1 (n.d.).

Richardson, H. W., *Input-Output and Regional Economics,* New York: John Wiley & Sons (1972).

Richardson, H. W., *Regional Growth Theory,* New York: Wiley (1973).

Rodgers, J., *State Estimates of Commodity Trade Flows,* Lexington, Mass.: Lexington Books (1973).

Rosen, H. and Mathur, V. "An Econometric Technique versus Traditional Techniques for Obtaining Regional Employment Multipliers," *Environment and Planning* 5:273–282 (1973).

Rowan, R. E., "Industry Employment Projections: An MRIO Model Simulation," prepared for the Massachusetts Division of Employment Security (1976).

Schaffer, W. A., *On the Use of Input-Output Models for Regional Planning,* Leiden: Martinus Nijhoff Social Sciences Division (1976).

Schaffer, W. A. and W. C. Biven, *The Impact of Georgia Tech.,* Atlanta, Ga.: Georgia Institute of Technology (1978).

Schaffer, W. A. and K. Chu, "Nonsurvey Techniques for Constructing Regional Interindustry Models," *Papers of the Regional Science Association* 23:83–101 (1969).

Schaffer, W. A., E. A. Laurent, and E. M. Sutter, Jr., *Using the Georgia Economic Model,* Atlanta, Ga.: College of Industrial Management, Georgia Institute of Technology (1972).

Schaffer, W. A. et at., *The Nova Scotia Input-Output System: 1974*, Halifax, Nova Scotia: Institute of Public Affairs, Dalhousie University (1977).

Simonovits, A., "A Note on the Underestimation and Overestimation of the Leontief Inverse," *Econometrica* 43:493–498 (1975).

Southwest Michigan Council of Governments (forthcoming).

Steiker, G., et al., *Richmond Input-Output Study: Volume II, Construction of the Richmond Model,* Regional Science Research Institute Report No. 50 (1976).

Stein, J. L., "Interregional Comparisons of the Marginal Product of Capital," *Southern Economic Journal,* 25:24–32 (1958).

Stevens, B., "Linear Programming and Location Rent," *Journal of Regional Science* 3:15–26 (1961).

Stevens, B. H., R. E. Coughlin, and C. Brackett, *An Investigation of Location Factors Influencing the Economy of the Philadelphia Region,* Philadelphia: Regional Science Research Institute (1967).

Stevens, B. H. and G. A. Trainer, "The Generation of Error in Regional Input-Output Impact Models," Regional Science Research Institute, Working Paper A1-76 (1976).

Stevens, B. H., et al., *Fore River Bridge Reconstruction Evaluation: Summary Report,* Office of Transportation Planning, Department of Public Works, Commonwealth of Massachusetts (1975).

Stilwell, F. J. and B. D. Boatwright, "A Method of Estimating Interregional Trade Flows," *Regional and Urban Economics* 1:77–87 (1971).

Theil, H., *Applied Economic Forecasting,* Amsterdam: North-Holland (1966).

Theil, H. and J. C. G. Boot, "The Final Form of Econometric Equation Systems," *Review of the International Statistical Institute* 30:136–152 (1962).

Thompson, G. E., "An Investigation of the Local Employment Multiplier," *Review of Economics and Statistics* 41:61–67 (1959).

Thompson, W., *A Preface to Urban Economics,* Baltimore, Md.: John Hopkins Press (1965).

Tiebout, C. M., *The Community Economic Base Study,* supplementary paper No. 16. New York: Committee for Economic Development (1962).

Transportation and Communications as Complementary Forces in Rural Development, Fairfield, Conn.: New Rural Society Project, Fairfield University (1976).

Treyz, G., *The Massachusetts Economic Policy Analysis Model,* Department of Economics, University of Massachusetts, Amherst, Massachusetts (1977).

Treyz, G., A. F. Friedlander, and B. H. Stevens, *A Regional Economic Policy Simulation Model,* working paper No. 202, Department of Economics, Massachusetts Institute of Technology (1978).

Ullman, E. L., "Minimum Requirements After a Decade: A Critique and an Appraisal," *Economic Geography* 44:364–369 (1968).

Ullman, E. L. and M. F. Dacey, "The Minimum Requirements Approach to the Urban Economic Base," *Papers and Proceedings of the Regional Science Association* 6:175–194 (1960).

Ullman, E., M. Dacey, and H. Brodsky. *The Economic Base of American Cities.* Seattle: University of Washington Press (1969).

U.S. Department of Labor, Bureau of Labor Statistics, *Factbook for Estimating the Manpower Needs of Federal Programs,* Bulletin No. 1832, Washington, D.C.: U.S. Government Printing Office (1975).

Von Thunen, J., *Von Thunen's Isolated State,* New York: Pergammon Press (1966).

Weber, A., *Alfred Weber's Theory of the Location of Industries,* Chicago: University of Chicago Press (1929).

Webster, R., et al., *The Economic Impact Forecast System: Descriptor and User Instructions,* Technical Report N-2, Champaign, Illinois: Construction Engineering Research Laboratory (1976).

Weiss, S. J. and E. C. Gooding, "Estimation of Differential Employment Multipliers in a Small Regional Economy," *Land Economics* 44:235–244 (1968).

Williamson, R. B., "Simple Input-Output Models for Area Economic Analysis," *Land Economics* 46:333–338 (1970).

Young, J. K., "The Multiregional Input-Output Price Model: Transportation Case Study," Ph.D. thesis (unpublished), Cambridge, Mass.: Massachusetts Institute of Technology (1978).

INDEX